To René David Osses

Ernest
Hemingway
Rediscovered

Norberto Fuentes

Ernest Hemingway
Rediscovered

**Photographs by
Roberto Herrera Sotolongo**

Translated from the French by
Marianne Sinclair

Charles Scribner's Sons   New York

Charles Scribner's Sons
Macmillan Publishing Company
866 Third Avenue, New York, NY 10022

Photographs by Roberto Herrera Sotolongo;
color photographs of the Finca Vigía
by Jean-Paul Paireault

Coordination: Zlatko Susic
Designed by Jacques Hennaux
Assisted by Sandrine Desbordes

Library of Congress Cataloging-in-Publication Data

Fuentes, Norberto.
Ernest Hemingway rediscovered.

Translation of: Ernest Hemingway retrouvé.
1. Hemingway, Ernest, 1899–1961 — Biography.
2. Novelists, American — 20th century — Biography.
I. Title.
PS3515.E37Z594313   1988   813′.52 [B]   88–15807
ISBN 0-684-18968-2

Macmillan books are available at special discounts for bulk purchases
for sales promotions, premiums, fund-raising, or educational use.
For details, contact:
Special Sales Director
Macmillan Publishing Company
866 Third Avenue
New York, NY 10022

10 9 8 7 6 5 4 3 2 1

Printed in Spain by Cronion s.a

Acknowledgements

I wish to thank all those who helped, sustained and encouraged me
throughout the various stages of the book. My special thanks to Carlos
Aldana, both for his help as a poet and as a critic. My eternal gratitude
must go to Max Marambio for his tireless enthusiasm.
Some contributions were particularly outstanding and deserve
special mention: the Copyright team in Paris (Hervé Tardy, Zlatko
Susic, Jacques Hennaux, Jean-Paul Paireault and Marina Zmak) and
the members of the International Network Group in Paris and in
Havana, Carlos Cadelo, Teodoro Espinosa, Eusebio Fernández,
Alcibiades Hidalgo, Sandro and Joan Gandini, José Antonio Gonzáles,
Una Liutkus, José Francisco Ordriozola, Miria Contreras and Lourdes
Guitart.
For their inexhaustible patience, generosity and help, my heartfelt
thanks to Raùl Rivero, Marilú Moré and Lourdes Curbelo.
Grateful thanks to: Jean-Claude Francolon who originally conceived
the project, Gladys Rodriquez Ferrero, director of the Hemingway
Museum in Havana and her staff.
Finally, I am indebted to Gloria Clavijo, Roberto Herrera Sotolongo's
widow, who kindly entrusted to us the invaluable photographs which
form the major part of this book.

CONTENTS

*T*he photographs in this book complete the life story of Ernest
Hemingway, shedding new and revealing light on the years he
spent in Cuba. It is highly unlikely that any other new visual
material of this importance will ever surface again because photographers
who have taken pictures of Hemingway have either already published
them or given them to his heirs. Many of these are now collected together
with Hemingway's files and papers at the John F. Kennedy Library in
Boston and the Firestone Library at Princeton University.

Most of the previously unpublished photographs in this volume were
taken by Roberto Herrera Sotolongo, a Spanish political exile living in
Cuba. Herrera was a keen amateur photographer, who used two cameras,
a 35mm Leica and a 120 Rolleiflex with a powerful flash called a Stereo
Viewmaster Realist. With this now antiquated equipment, he liked to take
photographs at birthdays and weddings or to do portraits of his relatives
and friends.

During the forties and fifties, Herrera belonged to the small, exclusive
circle of people who regarded themselves as the 'Hemingway set' in
Havana, a rough, tough bunch of unconventional cronies and dependants.
He possessed all the required qualities: he could knock back a double
unsweetened daiquiri with the best of them, he was a conscientious
worker, and he was as loyal as they came. From the early forties onwards
he was Hemingway's private secretary, as well as manager of the land
around Hemingway's house, Finca Vigía, at San Francisco de Paula near
Havana, and he claimed to have helped Hemingway prepare his accounts
for the taxman's eyes each year. Once he had been admitted to the
'veterans' brigade', he never left it. Nor did he ever stop taking pictures.
His photographs cover Hemingway's years of residence in Cuba from
1939 to 1960, and as the time passed he became an excellent
photographer. All his pictures are technically competent, well framed and
evocative.

After Hemingway's death, Finca Vigía became a museum and Roberto
Herrera Sotolongo was its first caretaker. Later he completed his medical
studies, which had been cut short by the Spanish Civil War, qualified as a

doctor in 1966 and practised at the Calixto Garcia General Hospital in Havana until he died of a heart attack in 1970.

Herrera was not only a good photographer. He was also a very modest one. Although some of his pictures were to become classics – such as the one of Hemingway and his fourth wife, Mary, on the flying bridge of the Pilar – he was never credited for them. Most of his work remained hidden away, unpublished, during his lifetime.

It was therefore an extraordinary stroke of luck that after Herrera's death in 1970, his widow, Gloria Clavijo happened to show me her husband's photographs to ask me whether there was 'anything to be got out of them'. I was at the time working on the massive task of reconstructing Hemingway's years in Cuba through his papers and through interviews with those people who had known him. These invaluable photographs had remained stashed in 'four yellow Kodak boxes', three of them on top of her bedroom wardrobe and another inside a chest in the living-room. She had had no idea of their real value, although she knew that her husband had always treasured them, and had often spent whole evenings pouring over them and re-organizing them in files.

So it was that I found myself in possession of this priceless collection of photographs. Some of the negatives had been slightly damaged over the years. The Cuban climate is particularly humid, and no one had ever taken any special precautions to preserve them. But they undoubtedly constituted the most extraordinary find since the author's death, a unique contribution to the Hemingway picture collection. They were not just the work of some professional, dispatched to take a random series of shots of the writer, but the day-to-day record of a man who had been very close to Hemingway, who had been his friend for over twenty years. They revealed every aspect of the Finca, each one of Papa's gang, his fishing expeditions, his hunting club, his favourite haunts in Havana, his women – in other words, his whole world. That, then, is the story of the Sotolongo photographs which form the major part of this work.

The remaining illustrations fall into two categories. Firstly, there are those that Hemingway himself kept at Finca Vigía and which illustrate Chapter One of this volume. Secondly, there are the specially commissioned colour photographs of the Finca as it looks today, taken by the French photographer Jean-Paul Pairault, and which illustrate the final section of this book.

Not a single photograph in Hemingway's private collection of photographs was preserved in an album. He attached no special importance to personal photographs, apart from Karsh's celebrated portrait of him and a few snapshots of family members which he slipped under the glass of his writing desk. The rest were kept in plain wooden boxes and were no better looked after than Sotolongo's collection. The only albums that Hemingway kept at Finca Vigía were scrapbooks containing newspaper clippings about his two plane crashes in Uganda in January 1954. It was initially concluded that he had died in the second disaster and his albums contain the consequent over-hasty obituaries, composed by so-called friends. In his autobiographical essay, 'The Christmas Gift', written as he recovered in Nairobi, he had half-indignantly and half-ironically announced that he would have the albums bound in lion and zebra skin. In fact, they remained bound in cardboard.

Hemingway's home at Finca Vigía has been preserved exactly as in the days when he lived there and remains a vivid moving evocation of the author's life, which the photographs in the final section of the book convey. Hemingway lived there for most of the last 22 years of his life, and it was the only settled permanent residence of his adult years. It is still filled with the sense of his presence. It is as if the man might walk into the room or down the path to the pool at any moment.

The last living witnesses of Hemingway's years in Cuba are fast disappearing: his younger brother, Leicester, died in 1982; his fourth wife, Mary in 1986; Adriana, his last great love, in 1983. His third wife, Martha Gellhorn, remains steadfastly silent... Some of the people who speak about him in these pages were simple people – neighbours, servants or friends no one has heard of – but amongst them are the celebrated *skipper of the* Pilar, *Gregorio Fuentes, a first-rate story-teller, and the laconic José Luis Herrera Sotolongo, Roberto's older brother, a friend of Fidel Castro, and Hemingway's private doctor, the man who looked after his health from 1940 until almost the end of his life.*

The purpose of this book is to recapture a little of Hemingway's personal warmth, a little of the sun-drenched life he loved to lead. The man who emerges from these photographs is the one most familiar to the 'Finca Vigía crowd' – in other words his Spanish Republican buddies, his servants, his friends and the fishermen of Cuba. A man who liked a peaceful existence and who enjoyed the simple things of life. A Hemingway who did not share his secrets and who had not many friends to share them with anyway. A sensitive, tragic, solitary individual who was, in some ways, the exact opposite of his legend.

Norberto Fuentes
Havana, 1987

CHAPTER ONE

BIOGRAPHICAL NOTES FOR AN ESSAY ON

THE SHORT HAPPY LIFE OF

ERNEST MILLER HEMINGWAY

KEY EVENTS: PERSONAL AND PUBLIC

AND HIS WORK

At Key West, around 1929, on the porch of his house. It was here at this time that Ernest Hemingway wrote A Farewell to Arms

How do you know what someone is like? You'll never get it right Because what you are judging is the past.

José Guimaraes Rosa

Ernest Miller Hemingway was born on 21 July 1899 in Oak Park, a suburb of Chicago, Illinois, at 439 North Oak Park Avenue. Oak Park was 'genteel, strait-laced and rigidly Protestant'. His father, Dr Clarence Edmonds Hemingway, was a fervent member of the First Congregational Church, and his mother, Grace Hall, sang in the church choir.

Grace Hall loved music; she had a good contralto voice and could have made a professional career as a singer. Her husband, a hard-working, successful doctor, preferred hunting and fishing. The education of their six children alternated between these two extremes. Ernest was given his first fishing-rod on his third birthday, a cello on his eighth birthday, and a shotgun when he turned ten.

The little boy stalked game with his shotgun round Bear Lake (later Walloon Lake) in northern Michigan, where the Hemingway family spent every summer. As far as Ernest was concerned, this valley was a paradise where he could walk bare-foot, run until he was breathless through the woods, and fish and hunt, far from the constricted atmosphere of his suburban home. Later, while he was still a student at Oak Park High, Ernest saw his first prize fight. He took up boxing and soon grew crazy about the sport.

In February 1916, Hemingway published his first literary work, 'Judgment of Manitou', the first of three stories, in *Tabula*, the school magazine. He also published several reports in the school's weekly, *Trapeze*. He had had the benefit of inspirational teaching – from Miss Fannie Briggs, who taught the Journalism course. When he graduated from Oak Park High the following year, he decided to earn his living as a reporter. College was a possibility but he wanted to work for a year first. A friend of his uncle's helped him find his first job – on the *Kansas City Star*. One of America's top newspapers, it had its own style handbook and Hemingway later acknowledged his debt to it: 'Those were the best rules I ever learned for the business of writing. I've never forgotten them.'

The United States entered the First World War on 6

Spain, March 1937, during the Civil War. Hemingway with Alexis Eisner, then lieutenant and later aide-de-camp to the Hungarian General Lucasz, at

Fuentes de Alcarria. With Ludwig Renn, he inspects a 'Cri-cri' captured from Franco's troops. A Cri-cri was an Italian machine used to tow pieces of ordnance.

With the American torero *Sidney Franklyn, who belonged to Hemingway's band of Republican friends. The castle of Manzanares appeared in the background of innumerable photographs of Hemingway during the Spanish Civil War.*

April 1917 and he tried in vain to sign up – but his left eye, defective from birth, disqualified him for military service. However, he enlisted in the Missouri National Guard once he reached Kansas and remained on the lookout for opportunities to get to the front. When he learned that the Red Cross was looking for ambulance drivers to go to Italy, he volunteered. He sailed for Europe on 23 May 1918 and was posted to northern Italy in early June. On the night of 8 July, at Fossalta on the Piave, Ernest was seriously injured by a shell fired from an Austrian trench mortar. With his own legs peppered with shrapnel, he carried one of his Italian companions to safety and received further wounds from enemy machine-guns.

'I died in that hole,' he was to say later, describing what had happened. But there were compensations. He fell in love with Agnes Hannah von Kurowsky, the nursing sister who looked after him in the American Red Cross Hospital in Milan. (She was to be the model for Catherine Barkley in *A Farewell to Arms.*) And he was awarded the *Medaglia d'argento al valore.*

But by January 1919, the great adventure was over. Ernest Hemingway was back home in Oak Park. He had earned a medal for valour but he had lost his sleep. He kept on having nightmares about death. Then, in March, Agnes threw him over for an aristocratic Italian lieutenant. Hemingway fell into a deep depression.

It was January 1920 before he took another job, as a tutor, and in February he began doing freelance human-interest stories for the *Star Weekly* in Toronto. In October 1920 he moved to Chicago, in December became assistant editor of a monthly published by the Cooperative Society and started to enjoy life again. He met the writer Sherwood Anderson and in September 1921 he married his first wife, Elizabeth Hadley Richardson. Encouraged by Anderson, they decided to go to Europe; Hemingway had a contract with the *Toronto Daily Star* to cover Europe and the Middle East.

They arrived in Paris on 22 December 1921, bearing

with them a letter of introduction from Sherwood Anderson to Gertrude Stein. Ernest liked her immediately and
dashed off a brief, pencilled note to Anderson, describing
their meeting: 'We love Gertrude Stein.' Gertrude Stein
was an important influence on Hemingway's work, en-
couraging him to concentrate on his literary output and
heightening his sensitivity.

But he met other literary expatriates in Paris who
taught him much about himself, about life and about the
art of writing, among them Sylvia Beach, James Joyce and
Wyndham Lewis. Ezra Pound became one of his best
friends, but at the same time he was a ruthless critic of
Ernest's work. Hemingway described their quarrels in an
ironic yet affectionate way: 'Ezra was right about half the
time; when he was wrong, he was so wrong that it was
completely apparent. But Gertrude Stein was never
wrong.'

The Hemingways lived reasonably well. Their Paris
apartment was cheap, but they went skiing and travelled
widely in northern Italy and Spain. Ernest's work for the
Star also took him to several international conferences
and to cover the aftermath of the Greco-Turkish War.
During the winter of 1922, Hadley lost a suitcase in the
Gare de Lyon: it was stolen from her railway carriage
while she checked the rest of her luggage. The case
contained not only their savings but Ernest's original
manuscripts *and* copies of a novel and a number of short
stories and poems. It was a personal disaster, of course,
but no one will ever know the literary value of these
unpublished works. Perhaps it forced the young writer to
start all over again on a sounder basis.

In the early summer of 1923, he went to Spain to
follow the bullfights for the first time, travelling all over
the country with a crew of *toreros*. In August, his first
book *Three Stories and Ten Poems* was published
privately in Paris in an edition of 300 copies, by the
Contact Publishing Company. And in the same month he
and Hadley returned to Canada. She was pregnant and

*Near the German border,
autumn 1944. Next to
Hemingway is 'Red'
Pelkey, his driver. A
Thompson sub-
machinegun is carefully
hidden between the front
seats of the Wyllis.*

On the plains of Serengeti in Africa. A rhinoceros has been tracked down. It hasn't yet noticed Hemingway.

distrusted Parisian hospitals. Hemingway visualized a two-year stay and took a full-time job with the *Star*. His first son, John Hadley Nicanor, (named after his favourite bullfighter) was born in October that year in Toronto, and on 31 December Hemingway resigned from the *Star*. The job and Toronto were suffocating, and on 19 January 1924 they were on their way back to Paris, where Hemingway planned to concentrate on his writing.

In 1924 he helped Ford Madox Ford edit the *Transatlantic Review* and worked mainly on his short stories and poems, but his approach was so new that he found it hard to get published. In the summer of 1925, he wrote the first draft of *The Sun Also Rises*, his first novel, and in October *In Our Time* was published commercially and hailed with enthusiasm by Scott Fitzgerald and D. H. Lawrence. His star was definitely rising, but his marital situation was rapidly deteriorating – he had grown bored with Hadley. In November he wrote *The Torrents of Spring*, a satirical attack on Sherwood Anderson which

disassociated him from his early mentor. In 1926 *The Torrents of Spring* and *The Sun Also Rises* were published by Scribners in New York. The latter established him as a major, influential American writer. From that time on, Scribners became his life-long publisher.

In February 1926 he had begun an affair with Pauline Pfeiffer, a wealthy, attractive, independent socialite, a woman vastly different from the increasingly domestic Hadley. That summer Hadley endured a *menage à trois*, then imposed a trial separation upon the lovers; she relented and admitted defeat before the 100 days was up. Although he loved Pauline, the parting from Hadley hurt Hemingway badly; he would always look upon divorce as a confession of failure, a personal defeat. He hated living alone. The idea of dying without a woman by his side terrified him. He once said: 'A man alone – even if he has been happy – dies in despair.' He married Pauline on 10 May 1927. In March 1928 Hemingway 'grabbed her by the middle' – which was the best way to handle a woman, he

The duel has begun. Hemingway has skill, intelligence and a good weapon on his side, not to mention courage. He will wait for the rhinoceros to charge and then will shoot only when it is close enough to be killed with a single shot.

Photographs of
Hemingway's second
African safari, 1953–4,
taken by Earl Theisen
for Look magazine.
Hemingway was always
conscious of his public
image and therefore
rejected the first
photograph, in which,
with an incongruous
smile, he contemplates
the animal he has just
brought down. He
agreed to the five other
prints being
published.

On another day the Masai warrior gives Hemingway a demonstration of the correct handling of the spear. He spent the entire morning learning the art of throwing and that evening showed his dexterity by killing two monkeys with this new weapon.

21

*Uganda, January, 1954. A few dollars change
hands . . . and the warriors' sharp arrows become
yet another of Hemingway's trophies.*

always insisted – and dragged her off to Key West, a tiny island off the tip of Florida.

Literary life in Paris was losing its sparkle, and Key West was the ideal place to relax. You could hunt and fish there; the air was clean and the sun shone most of the time. Ernest did a lot of boxing, swimming and walking to keep in trim. He also met two characters who were to play an important part both in his life and in his work. During one of his first outings in the Gulf Stream, he came across a certain Captain Eddie 'Bra' Saunders, who had looted a Spanish galleon. Eddie taught him deep-sea fishing and gave him the idea for a novella, *After the Storm*. Subsequently, he met Joe Russell, who owned two of the things Ernest was to love best: a bar, Sloppy Joe's, and a boat, the *Anita*.

That June, in Kansas City, Pauline gave birth to Hemingway's second son, Patrick, and in October he published a volume of short stories, *Men Without Women*. By the end of November they were back in Key West, and Hemingway had completed the first draft of the novel *A Farewell to Arms*. He seemed very contented. Pauline, who had worked for French *Vogue* before their marriage, had happily given up her career to be a full-time wife and mother. The year 1928 had been a good one for Hemingway, both in his private and in his professional life; but it ended tragically. On 6 December he learned that his father had committed suicide.

The suicide and its aftermath heightened the bitterness he always felt towards his mother, but he forced himself to concentrate on the revision of *A Farewell to Arms* and then he and Pauline travelled through Europe for the rest of the year, returning to Key West in January 1930. *A Farewell to Arms* had come out in September 1929 and its first printing of 31,000 copies sold out

immediately. It was a critical success too and brought him to the high point of his career.

When the hurricane season hit Key West, he went north to hunt and fish in Wyoming. It was there, on 1 November 1930, that he had the first of a long succession of car and plane crashes. He was hospitalized at Billings, Montana. During his seven-week convalescence, he let his beard grow and was delighted with the effect it produced on the startled Pauline: the beard made him look older, but also wiser and more respectable.

Pauline was pregnant again in February 1931, but that did not stop them travelling to Spain and France. Hemingway's youngest son, Gregory Hancock, nicknamed Gigi, was born in Kansas City in November 1931. Just before Christmas the family moved into a large, colonial-style house on Whitehead Street in Key West, bought by Pauline's uncle. Here Hemingway finished *Death in the Afternoon*, his comprehensive study of bullfighting. Published in September 1932, the book sold well initially, but it earned his first unfavourable reviews, including Max Eastman's famous 'Bull in the Afternoon' article.

It was in the early thirties that the legendary Hemingway persona made its appearance. He found it difficult to handle the publicity his fame inevitably attracted. Gertrude Stein once said of him: 'He had compensated for his incredibly acute shyness and sensitivity by adopting a shield of brutality.' And she added: 'When this happened he lost touch with his genius.'

During 1932 and 1933 Hemingway began making regular trips to Cuba, frequently on fishing expeditions with Joe Russell off the northern coast of the island. They established their headquarters at the Ambos Mundos Hotel in Havana, near the Floridita bar, where Hemingway was a regular.

The merciless sun of Africa caused Hemingway's sensitive skin to peel. His beard gave him some protection, but he was always anxious about his skin's condition, which his Cuban doctor diagnosed as 'a mild case of melanosis'.

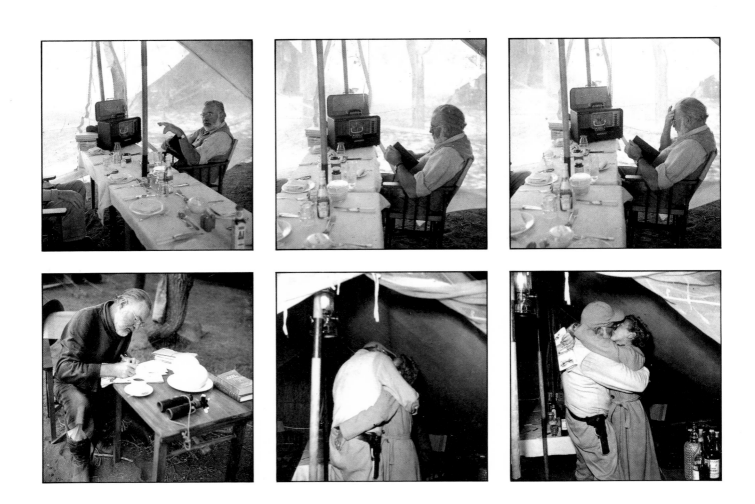

More photographs of Hemingway's second African safari, 1953–4, taken by Earl Theisen for Look magazine. Hardly 'death in the afternoon'. Hemingway whiles away the early evening by reading, listening to broadcasts from the BBC,

writing up his journals, and sharing an
affectionate moment with Mary.
A day spent hunting with the Masai. A lion's age
is revealed by its teeth. This one is an adult male.

A quay at Cojímar, near Havana, around 1929. Hemingway has caught a marlin weighing about 500 pounds. He is holding a Tycoon split-bamboo rod, which was fashionable at that time. Next to him is Carlos Gutiérrez, who was briefly the skipper of Hemingway's boat, the Pilar. Gutiérrez is said to have been one of the models for Santiago, the hero of The Old Man and the Sea.

The writer took a keen interest in the Cuban people's struggle against the dictator Gerardo Machado. During the summer of 1933 Hemingway caught his first really big fish. He had given up journalism ten years before, but now he started writing a series of articles on hunting and fishing for *Esquire*. He was also writing the short stories published to hostile reviews under the title *Winner Take Nothing* in October 1933.

He and Pauline were in Europe and Africa from August 1933 to March 1934. They spent the New Year in Africa and went on safari on the Serengeti plain. The safari got off to a bad start: Hemingway had an attack of amoebic dysentry and had to be rushed back to Nairobi. As soon as he recovered, he rejoined the party and bagged three lions and almost 30 other animals. On his return to Key

West in the spring, he built his own boat, the *Pilar*, and began work on *Green Hills of Africa*, his personal account of big-game hunting. Meanwhile, the first part of the Harry Morgan saga, 'One Trip Across', was printed in *Cosmopolitan* in April 1934.

In 1935 he won his first fishing contest at Bimini in the British West Indies. Foreigners were unpopular at Bimini, and Hemingway's victory provoked a number of quarrels. He decided to give the local fishermen a chance to vent their ill-feelings and offered $200 to the man who could stay in the ring with him for four rounds. No one managed to get hold of the prize money. On another occasion, he had an epic fist-fight with Tom Heeney, the British big-game fishing champion, on a beach, before a crowd of enthusiastic onlookers. After a few rounds, Hemingway

Hemingway with his fishermen friends, bringing in the dragnet on the north coast of Cuba, around 1955. These dragnets are used to catch bait: this is not fishing for sport, but part of the hard traditional work of men who earn their living from the sea.

said to his opponent: 'The hell with it! We're not even getting paid! We should at least be getting a few dollars for putting on such a show.'

That year, he published an article in the September issue of the Communist journal *New Masses* titled 'Who Murdered the Vets?' It exposed the needless death of hundreds of war veterans in the Matecumbe Keys during the tremendous hurricane that had devastated the area on 2 September 1935. *Green Hills of Africa* came out in October 1935, and again the reviews were unfavourable. The following February, *Esquire* printed 'The Trademan's Return', the sequel to the Harry Morgan story. Later in 1936 Hemingway's best and favourite stories of Africa came out: 'The Snows of Kilimanjaro' and 'The Short Happy Life of Francis Macomber'.

Then in December 1936 Hemingway met the journalist and writer Martha Gellhorn at Sloppy Joe's. It was a mutual, instant attraction. Both of them tried to keep the affair secret, but they began planning to go to the Spanish Civil War together. Hemingway was to make four trips there as war correspondent for the N.A.N.A. (the North American Newspapers Alliance) between March 1937 and November 1938. Martha met him in Madrid in March 1937; she was working for *Collier's* magazine. They became lovers and, as Martha put it: 'He's a romantic by nature and falls in love very suddenly and deeply. There's a puritanical side to his nature which makes him dislike flirting. When he's in love, his greatest wish is to get married.'

During his first trip to Spain – between March and May

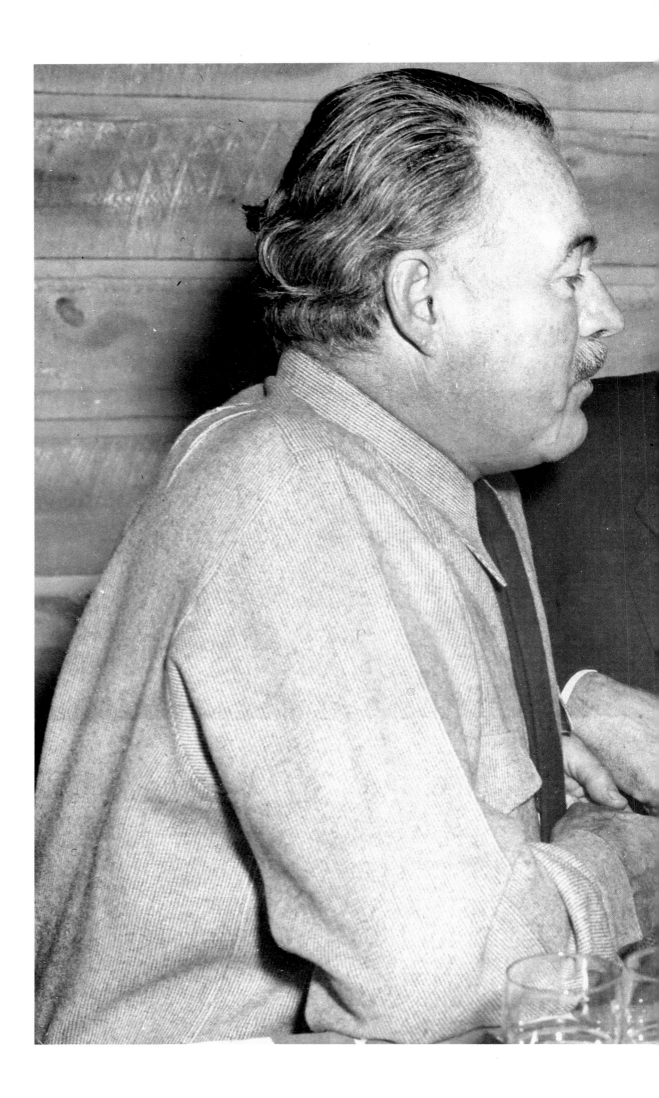

Sun Valley, Idaho,
10 January 1948.
Hemingway meets up
with Gary Cooper and
Ingrid Bergman during a
winter-sports holiday. He
had first got to know them
when they starred in the
film For Whom the Bell
Tolls.

1937 – he took part in the filming of the documentary *The Spanish Earth*. On his return to the United States, Hemingway made his first political speech – at Carnegie Hall on 4 June 1937, before the League of American Authors Congress – and went to Hollywood to raise funds for the purchase of ambulances for the Spanish Republicans. He put the finishing touches to the Harry Morgan novel, *To Have and Have Not*, in June 1937 – the previous year he had written a third part – and then he set off once more for Spain. The book was published in the autumn and collected bad reviews, but it sold 36,000 copies in the first five months. He wrote his only play, *The Fifth Column*, while his Madrid hotel was under fire in the autumn of 1937.

By the time he left Spain in November 1938, Hemingway's second marriage was in ruins, but it was September 1939 before he and Pauline finally separated. Again, he was suffering agonies of guilt. In this atmosphere he began to write *For Whom the Bell Tolls*. Much of it was written on the move: some of it at the Ambos Mundos Hotel in Havana and at Finca Vigía, a house which he and Martha rented in April 1939, outside the city. The novel came out in October 1940 to critical acclaim; it sold 500,000 copies in the first five months, and with the money Hemingway bought his Cuban house, Finca Vigía.

He got a divorce from Pauline and married Martha Gellhorn on 21 November 1940. But when they set off for the Far East to cover Chiang Kai-Shek's war against Japan in January 1941 their relationship was already strained. Hemingway was finding it hard to accept just how important Martha's career was to her. She had accepted the assignment from *Collier's* so he fixed himself up with the newspaper *PM*. The trip to China temporarily eased their difficulties, but when he returned to Cuba he began to drift. With Martha often away – she was a reporter in wartime England for some time – he spent more and more time fishing, enjoying his Cuban friendships, and hunting in Sun Valley, Idaho, his new autumn home.

Then, in August 1942, with the States now Britain's ally in the Second World War, Hemingway created the Crook Factory, a private undertaking whose self-appointed mission was to investigate the pro-Nazi factions in Cuba. Its headquarters were at Finca Vigía and until April 1943 its undercover agents – fishermen, priests, waiters, pimps, and whores – collected information on the Spanish Falangists on the island. The organization was finally disbanded and Hemingway concentrated all his efforts on 'sub-hunting'. The idea was to identify and to harrass any German submarines that might be lurking in the area.

Manuel Bell, a Cuban known to every fisherman across the Gulf Stream as Blacamàn, later recalled: 'Papa turned his boat into an armoured destroyer, and he would inspect the coast as far as Camagüey, as well as the eastern

keys right into the Mexican Gulf.' Hemingway would be on his boat day and night. When he ran out of food or fuel, he returned to Havana, stocked up and set off again.

This sport continued sporadically until March 1944; in May he arrived in London on assignment as war correspondent for *Collier's*: Martha had been urging him to play a more immediate role in the conflict. Soon after he arrived, he was involved in a serious car accident, and was reported dead by several newspapers. It was also in London in May 1944 that he met and fell in love with Mary Welsh. Martha had joined him in London but things were very bad between them.

Between June and December 1944, Hemingway covered the European conflict for the magazine. Officially, he was attached to the Third Army, but he also went out on reconnaissance and bombing raids with the RAF, and as he followed the Fourth Infantry Division's advance across Normandy in August, he refused to remain merely an onlooker. His articles became a pretext to remain at the front.

'How come a man of your age and intelligence, with so many battle-scars on him, has only a captain's rank?' asked one of the French Resistance fighters he met.

'Look, *mon vieux*, I'll tell you the simple and painful truth. I just never learned to read and write,' replied Hemingway.

Eventually, he was so involved in the business of fighting that the army was forced to court martial him for violating the Geneva Convention. (He was also awarded the Bronze Star for his services as a war correspondent in 1947.) His name cleared – with the help of some careful use of the truth – Hemingway rejoined Colonel Lanham and the Fourth Infantry Division and was with them for the fierce fighting in the Hurtgenwald in November– December 1944.

By early January 1945 he was back in Paris with Mary Welsh. His third marriage was effectively over and Mary was making up her mind whether or not to marry him. He did not stay in Europe to see the Armistice, but returned to Finca Vigía in March 1945 after a brief stop-over in New York. Mary joined him there but he was having trouble readjusting to peace and the pain of yet another failed marriage, and one night in June, after too many daiquiris at the Floridita, he had another serious car crash on the way home to the Finca. On 14 March 1946, with the divorce through he married Mary Welsh. She was the daughter of a Minnesota lumber-dealer, and had gone to Northwestern University before working for the *Chicago Daily News* as a society reporter.

In 1946 he started work on two projects: *The Garden of Eden* (published in 1986) and the first part of his proposed World War Two trilogy (published after his death as *Islands in the Stream*). His health was deteriorat-

At the helm of the Pilar, *around 1949. The Gulf Stream is calm and Hemingway surveys the horizon. His experiences as sailor, fisherman and war-time 'captain' were the inspiration for much of his writing.*

ing and his drinking had increased. Progress was difficult and slow. From 1947 to 1952 some of the people who had been closest to Hemingway were to die: first, his editor Maxwell Perkins; then his mother; then Pauline Pfeiffer and his publisher Charles Scribner. And his second son, Patrick, suffered a serious illness in 1947. He continued to write and also did a bit of conspiring against the Dominican dictator, Trujillo: in October 1947, an entire police squadron descended on Finca Vigía and confiscated all his firearms.

The Hemingways set off on a trip to northern Italy in September 1948, and he revisited the places to which he had been posted in 1918. In December, during a hunting party, he met and fell in love with the young and beautiful Adriana Ivancich.

He was back in Cuba for the summer of 1949 but was in Europe again from November to March 1950. And he was writing. *Across the River and Into the Trees*, the novel Adriana had inspired, was panned by reviewers when it came out in September 1950. Adriana and her mother arrived for a three-month stay at the Finca soon afterwards and were embarrassed by the publicity associated with the book. A bitter and despondent Hemingway resumed work on the first part of his war trilogy, putting it aside to write the novella *The Old Man and the Sea*, which he completed

just after Adriana left Cuba. It was published in book form in September 1952, restoring his popularity as a writer, getting rave reviews, and becoming a best-seller. The story of Santiago, the old fisherman, also won him the Pulitzer Prize in May 1953.

The following month the Hemingways sailed for Europe and spent some time in Spain – Hemingway was planning an appendix to *Death in the Afternoon* – before travelling on to Mombasa and his second safari. *Look* magazine was paying him handsomely for an article and a picture story, to be shot by Earl Theisen. He didn't enjoy the assignment and took time out to go 'native', conducting the ritual courtship of Debba, a young Wakamba girl. His long succession of car and plane accidents continued. Twice in January 1954 planes carrying him and Mary crashed and on the second occasion the newspapers announced his death. From his hospital bed in Nairobi, after the second, much more serious incident, he sent a telegram echoing Mark Twain's famous words to the press: 'The reports of my death are greatly exaggerated.' Only partly recovered from his injuries, he returned to Cuba in July via Venice (where he met Adriana for the last time) and Spain.

On 28 October 1954, Hemingway was awarded the Nobel Prize for Literature. A crowd of Cuban friends

Cuba, 1955. With Spencer Tracy, scouting for locations for the film The Old Man and the Sea.

New Year's Eve at the Floridita bar, Havana, 1951. At midnight, Gary Cooper ventures the traditional greeting: 'Happy New Year, Ernesto'. 1952 was indeed a happy year, at least for Hemingway the writer: on 8 September The Old Man and the Sea *was published to great acclaim. In the centre of the photograph, to the right of Hemingway, is his driver Juan Pastor, who would regularly deposit his intoxicated boss back at Finca Vigía after a heavy drinking session at the Floridita, Hemingway's favourite watering hole.*

28 October 1954. Havana society celebrates Hemingway's Nobel Prize. At midday there had been an informal celebration at Finca Vigía with the fishermen from Cojímar and the inhabitants of San Francisco de Paula.

With Mary in Venice in 1949. By now he was deeply in love with the young Italian countess Adriana Ivancich, who was the inspiration for Renata *in* Across the River and Into the Trees.

Finca Vigía, 1954. The Swedish ambassador to Cuba pays a courtesy visit after Hemingway has been awarded the Nobel Prize for Literature.

Finca Vigía, 1954. United States airmen, winners of the Airman of the Month award, visit Hemingway at his house, part of their reward for good behaviour during their period of service.

invaded Finca Vigía. He welcomed them with jokes, drinks and a huge buffet lunch. Afterwards, he made a speech: 'You know, there isn't just one Cuba but several Cubas. As in ancient Gaul, one can divide the island into three categories of people: those who don't get enough to eat, those who do get enough to eat, and those who overeat. After this lovely luncheon, there is little doubt that we belong to the third category, at least for the time being.' He ended by declaring that he would give his Nobel medal to the shrine of the national saint, the Virgen de la Caridad del Cobre, adding that no one could steal the $35,000 prize from him for the good reason that he hadn't yet received it.

By now he was deeply depressed by the slowness of his recovery; he was often in terrible pain, so he asked the US Ambassador to Sweden to collect his prize and sent a short address to the Swedish Academy instead: 'Writing, at its best, is a lonely life. Organizations for writers palliate the writer's loneliness but I doubt if they improve his writing. He grows in public stature as he sheds his loneliness and often his work deteriorates. For he does his work alone and if he is a good enough writer he must face eternity, or the lack of it, each day.' He gave a big party for his friends at the Finca on the day the ceremony was held in Stockholm.

During the mid 1950s his working life was spent writing short stories and his long African journal, neither of which he judged fit for publication, and becoming involved in the filming of *The Old Man and the Sea*. He was in Europe from September 1956 to January 1957, and he set sail again for Spain in May 1959, a month after Fidel Castro's troops entered Havana. He had a commission from *Life* magazine to write a series of articles on bullfighting entitled 'The Dangerous Summer'. When he

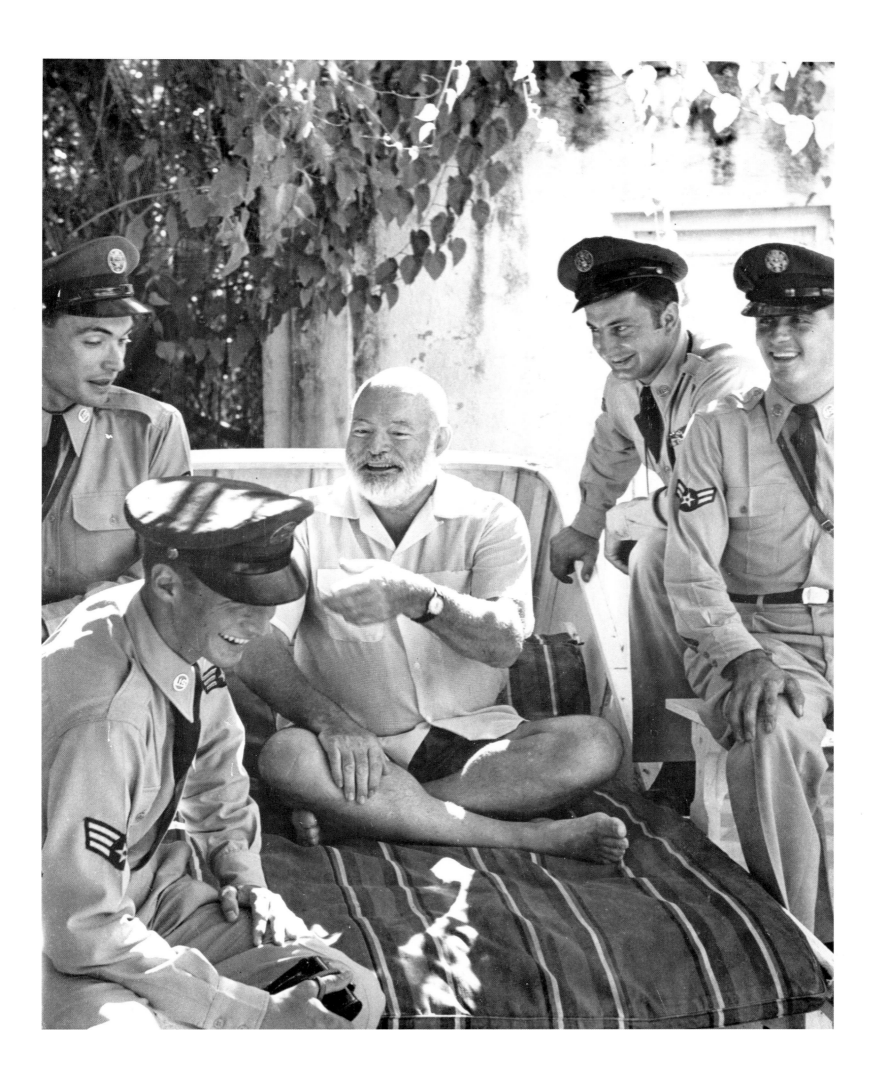

Hemingway and Mary introduce Spencer Tracy
to the pleasures of Havana's Floridita bar in
September 1955. The filming of The Old Man
and the Sea *had begun on the beach at Cojímar,*
just outside the city, but they failed to catch a fish
as large as Santiago's.

His last hunting trip with Gary Cooper, in Idaho in the winter of 1958–9. The actor asked his friend: 'How much do you want to bet that I'll die before you?' He won the wager, dying a month before Hemingway.

returned to Havana in early November, he publicly declared his support for the revolutionaries.

In the spring of 1960 he completed his memoir of life in Paris in the early twenties: *A Moveable Feast*. He had been working on it since the autumn of 1957. He met Castro in May 1960, during a fishing contest that had been named after him. Photographs taken on this occasion show them chatting but there is no record of what was said. All we know is that Castro invited Hemingway to go trout-fishing with him in a lagoon south east of Cuba, and that Hemingway accepted the invitation.

Hemingway left Cuba for the last time in July 1960. He was already showing signs of mental illness, his health had collapsed and he was forced to rely more and more on alcohol. In August he went to Spain alone but he cut his trip short to return to Ketchum, Idaho. On 30 November, he was admitted to the Mayo Clinic for the first time; he was released on 22 January 1961, re-admitted on 25 April and released again on 26 June. While in the clinic, he

underwent gruelling electric shock treatment and after his first confinement he found his memory had gone and he couldn't write any more. On the morning of 2 July 1961, he tripped the trigger of his double-barrelled shotgun and was instantly killed.

In Paris, during the twenties, Hemingway wrote a poem called 'Montparnasse'. It begins as follows:

No suicide is real.
A young Chinese boy killed himself and is dead.
(His mail still arrives at the Dôme).

Under the glass top of a table at the Finca Vigía visitors can see hundreds of unopened letters from all parts of the world.

He killed himself and is dead.

He still gets mail at Finca Vigía.

With Mary at Ketchum, Idaho, around 1946–7. Hemingway liked to go north to avoid the hurricane season. After he parted from Pauline, his second wife, Idaho replaced Wyoming as his mainland base: the hunting and fishing were equally good.

CHAPTER TWO

A GUIDING PRINCIPLE TO LIVE LIFE BY

GRACE UNDER PRESSURE

BUT ONE WHICH IMPOSES ITS OWN

PRESSURES

At the entrance to Finca Vigía, at the end of the forties. The cats and the ceiba tree which formed part of the writer's daily surroundings were later immortalized in Islands in the Stream.

A composition that Miró would have approved of. But what title would Miró, who was one of Hemingway's favourite painters, have given it?

Hemingway with one of his dogs at Finca Vigía, around 1954. In spite of his predilection for big-game hunting and fishing, Hemingway was a great animal lover and nursed any wounded animal that found its way into his garden.

A look which could be mistaken for arrogance, but it was probably the formidable combination of half a dozen daiquiris and a generous glassful of Scotch. On an average day, three or four friends could help Ernest consume three or four bottles of whisky. It never seemed to be too much for him.

Nowhere does Hemingway appear truer to his nature than in the photographs that show him hunting or fishing or on the battlefield. Whether he holds the Tycoon rod he used to catch spearfish or the Austrian Mannlicher Schoenaur .256 which he carried on elephant hunts, these images seem to encapsulate a truth. They show the Hemingway we remember: a bearded giant of a man in bermuda shorts and worn-out loafers, an instantly recognizable larger-than-life hero of our times.

There is a well-known photograph of him, taken from above as he sits in his convertible Wyllis, wearing a helmet and a mud-spattered, badgeless uniform. It was the winter of 1944. Hemingway was following the US Fourth Infantry Division as it pressed on towards the German frontier. His driver was a red-headed tearaway called Archie 'Red' Pelkey, from Potsdam, New York, who had dropped everything to enlist. General Raymond Oscar Barton had teamed him with Hemingway with instructions to keep the war correspondent safe – and not too close to the battle-zones. At first, the two men had used a Mercedes-Benz captured from the Germans soon after D-Day; now they had commandeered a brand-new Wyllis jeep.

Such pictures seem to confirm the Hemingway legend.

But, in fact, they conceal one aspect of the truth: under the mud-stains and the big smile is a man suffering bitter frustration.

For a start, picture him on his way to the Hurtgenwald, one of the principal Nazi defence lines, between Aachen and Bonn, carrying no weapon. His Thompson machine-gun no longer lies across his lap as it had a few weeks earlier. There had been a judicial investigation in the interim regarding his conduct as a war correspondent and it is better for him to keep his machine-gun hidden under the front seat of the jeep. Under the Geneva Convention, war correspondents are supposed to be neutral, and Hemingway had to appear before an army council at Nancy on 6 October on charges that he was in violation of those regulations. Specifically, it was alleged that at Rambouillet, 23 miles south west of Paris, he had 'stripped off his correspondent's insignia and acted as a colonel of French Resistance Troops; that he had a room with mines, grenades and war maps; that he directed Resistance patrols...'

Three testimonials and some carefully worded statements of his own had got him off the hook. Once he had been cleared, he roared with laughter, declaring that he

A modern god on the Gulf Stream.

would have the text of the Convention tattooed on his back so as never to forget it in future. But he knew that he was under threat of repatriation if he was seen to disobey, and in private he ranted against the 'contemptible orders of the ginebra Gordon' – a pun on Gordon's gin and the word ginebra, which means both 'gin' and 'Geneva' in Spanish. What made it even harder for Hemingway to put up with the 'contemptible Geneva rules' was that vital supplies of Gordon's gin were fast drying up as he neared the front.

It was agony for him to appear gunless while his buddies were fighting it out with the enemy. Nor was it any fun to have an ambitious, antagonistic wife working as a war correspondent with the Allied armies in the same

zone. Hemingway's third marriage, to Martha Gellhorn, was in serious difficulties long before they went to Europe in the Spring of 1944. He had loved her passionately but was unable to support the knowledge that she would never be prepared to make him the centre of her life, as his first two wives had done. Later he was to sum up that essential dilemma with the words, 'I need a wife in bed and not in the most widely circulated magazines.' When he met Mary Welsh in London in late May 1944, he began to consider the possibility of life without Martha but he did not find it easy to end the relationship. Torn between Martha Gellhorn and Mary Welsh, Hemingway was involved in a painful sentimental imbroglio which was a constant source of worry to him.

Hemingway regarded the sea as a peaceful sanctuary as well as a battleground. After a hard day's fishing he would go for a relaxing swim around the beaches east of Havana.

A third, even deeper, source of frustration for him was that his literary production had dwindled almost to nothing. As a writer, as opposed to a journalist, his career seemed to have come to a halt. And everyone was more or less aware of the fact. His past achievements must have seemed like an immense wall that he would have to try to scale once again, without help from anyone.

Life demanded that he play the tough guy to the end. And tough guys must obey certain rules, even if their personal code is almost certainly based on falsehood and the results are illusory. Some people admire that code; others find it absurd. William Faulkner, novelist and friend, once said that Hemingway's characters are all 'self-made, born of their own clay'; their achievements and their failures depend on them alone and are 'only intended to prove how tough they are'.

And yet the adrenalin was not pumping into his bloodstream all the time. Even tough guys need a rest once in a while. Between the physical and emotional tribulations, there were moments of respite. Hemingway found relief in somewhat heavy-handed horseplay, punning and practical jokes.

There was, for example Hemingway the hunter, deep in the African bush, trying to strike up a conversation with a herd of reticent but obviously foul-tempered elephants; Hemingway the writer, solemnly declaring in an interview for a very serious publication, *La Revue de Paris*, that Ezra Pound's name was a pseudonym for St. Elizabeth's Hospital.

In a long letter to Mary Welsh, dated 16–20 November 1944, Hemingway described the bitter fighting around the Hurtgenwald. The Germans were putting up a formidable show of resistance against the Fourth Division, during what was to be their last winter campaign: 'The Krauts are beaten and we only have to destroy this crust – But it is like facing the pitching of an old Pitcher who knows everything and has 4 fine innings in his arm – or an old boxer who can go 4 of 10 rounds – or even six.'

It was in this context that Hemingway decided to try out a new invention. The trials were carried out in a ruined farm near the Hurtgenwald, a precarious shelter for his audience, which consisted of members of 'Task Force Hemingway', including Colonel Lanham and Archie Pelkey. The group already enjoyed a thoroughly bad reputation as diehard iconoclasts throughout the Fourth

Hemingway inaugurates the wide porch at Finca Vigía in 1941, the year after he bought the house for $18,500. The satisfied smile and the glass in his hand conceal a man buffeted by the matrimonial squalls which would soon distance him from his third wife, Martha Gellhorn.

Not the best angle, nor perhaps the most dignified, but we can always recognize Hemingway at work. He wrote standing up, in bermuda shorts, shirtless, often barefoot, or else wearing moccasins or sandals, and with a bottle of Vichy water by his side.

Division, but most of all in the opinion of the division leader General Barton.

Hemingway's deadly weapon was an improvised 'mortar' comprising a length of stove-pipe at the top and a toilet seat at the base; the projectiles were champagne corks. Hemingway managed to hit a cigarette held at arm's length by the cook, and Pelkey, behind the ear, though he had warned him of the potential danger. He was thrilled by his success. Such childish horseplay was a way of feeling alive, of escaping the much harsher reality of their situation.

Even his plane accidents in Africa, both in January 1954, offered the opportunity for humour. It was a way of handling a situation others would have found embarrassing. Hemingway was seriously injured after the second crash and had a pretty rough time with 'a broken spine', or so he claimed. With two cracked discs compressing his sphinctal muscle, he boasted he had a permanent erection. More seriously, he had no bowel movement for 22 days. On the twenty-third, he recovered – and managed to excrete what looked like hard, white golf-balls. This greatly amused him, and the condition continued for some time, with him claiming to have passed up to 62 of them daily from a standing position. But on one occasion he missed the lavatory bowl and his wife said to him: 'Didn't you know that gentlemen don't do it on the ground?' In a letter to his British publisher, Jonathan

Cape, Hemingway records his proud reply: 'Well, aren't you lucky to know one who does?'

Hemingway also loved nicknames, and invented them for many of the people he knew. He also liked his own *nombretes*, as they are called in Spanish, and there were a lot of them, including Ernie, Hem, Wemedge, Dr. Heminstein, Ernest Hemorrhoid and Papa, his favourite, which, according to legend, was invented by Marlene Dietrich.

The latter is now widely used: when it appears on book and magazine covers, it improves sales. But many people who read neither books nor magazines also knew him as Papa. They called him Papa in the cosy little bars of Havana. So did the smugglers and fishermen off the coast of Cuba, Bimini and Florida and the Resistance fighters in Paris and elsewhere.

Of all his wives, Martha was the one who protected his private life with the most determination. He often resented the curiosity of those journalists, photographers and individuals who hounded him remorselessly. But unfortunately he had one weak spot: he loved to tell stories and would get completely carried away when he was given the chance to make some joke or describe an adventure of which he was, naturally, always the hero.

Equally, the hack writing he had to do for money – usually magazine articles – turned him into a well-known 'character'. As far as he was concerned, journalism was a

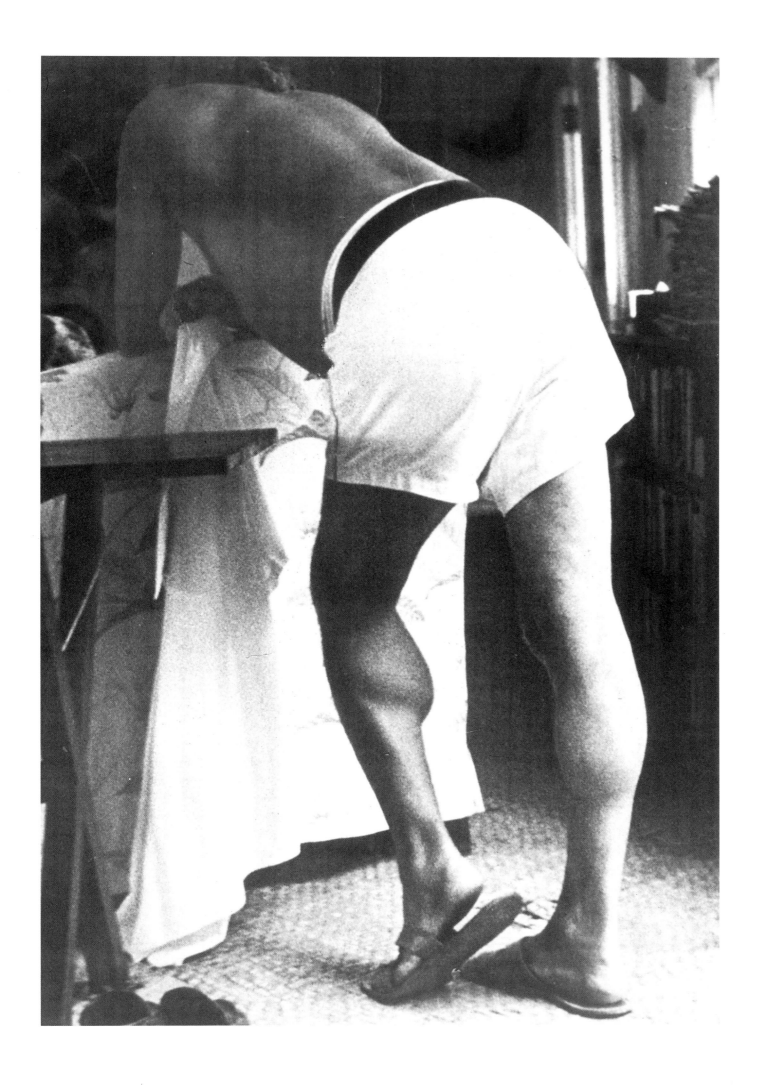

A Latin siesta for the demi-god of American literature. Hemingway has been working since dawn on the draft of Across the River and Into the Trees. *He would often nap until four or five o'clock in the afternoon at Finca Vigía.*

way for him to get to the places he wanted to go with all expenses paid – and generously. When he was commissioned to do an article, a photographer was frequently sent along with him, and these included such notable figures as Robert Capa and Earl Theisen. He would return from such assignments in a blaze of glory – and with endless reels of photographs of himself. All that remained was to sit down at his writing-table, boast of his exploits, select the photographs which showed him to best advantage, and hang up his trophies.

In such ways the Hemingway legend grew and grew until it reached heroic proportions. Hemingway the man is to be found elsewhere – in the snapshots of him taken by his friends, in their anecdotes about him, in the letters he wrote, and above all in his literary works.

Even early on in his career, critics contributed to the creation of the 'author-as-hero' legend. They looked for the man in his writings and had no trouble finding him there. Philip Young was the first to notice the close links which existed between photographs of the writer and the circumstances described in his works. He ran into a lot of trouble trying to finish his study of Hemingway, to which

the author was fiercely opposed. Young's central theory, that Hemingway's work derived from the trauma of the war wound he suffered in 1918, was supported by extensive quotation from the books. For a long time Hemingway refused to grant permission to quote. The editor of the book had to intercede, claiming that Young's livelihood was threatened, before publication could proceed.

I once spent an evening with the writer William Kennedy, on a beach called Cojímar, close to Havana. It is here that Santiago, the hero of *The Old Man and the Sea*, arrives with the remains of the enormous marlin still attached to the side of his boat. Waves crashed upon the sand, Kennedy gazed at the darkened beach so full of memories of Hemingway, and said: 'He would grab things. He would grab at anything within his grasp, everything he knew...'

Hemingway used whatever material came to hand. Sometimes, he went too far. On one occasion, for example, he visited Ring Lardner's son in a Spanish hospital and then immediately wrote a touching story about a great man visiting a wounded young American

The solitude of Puerto Escondido, 35 miles east of Havana, provided Hemingway with a good place for peace and tranquility.

On the Pilar *with his fourth wife, Mary.*

who has fought heroically in the Civil War. The boy greets the famous writer and begs him for advice; the writer is kind but remote as he tries to restore the young man's courage. We are moved by his concern until we recall that Hemingway is describing an event in which he has just participated.

Contemporary poets and writers did much to enhance the heroic figure they saw in the making. Archibald MacLeish looked upon Hemingway as a man of nature, who 'hews a style for his age out of a walnut tree'. Scott Fitzgerald, in one of his letters, emphasized Hemingway's iconoclastic approach to high-flown language: 'I hear you've written a book that has a succession of paragraphs completely built around the word "balls".'

Others saw in him the embodiment of the American Dream, but that was really beside the point. He was more like the harbinger of a certain concept of freedom. He could not stand wearing a tuxedo – even to receive the Nobel Prize. He felt much more at ease with the Spanish Republicans and the French *Maquisards*. With them, he could grin for photographs, relaxed, looking very pleased with himself, and brimming over with enthusiasm. He was a literary tycoon, a free man hacking his way through the dense thickets of American letters.

Freedom, wide-open spaces, travel, the sea, boats, guns, fighting: all these things were in Hemingway's blood. We know his father taught him to fish and to hunt – and later committed suicide with a shotgun. We know his paternal grandfather, Anson Taylor Hemingway, thrilled his small grandson with terrifying tales of the Civil War. Anson had served as a lieutenant of infantry in the Confederate Army. We know Alexander Hancock, his mother's grandfather, was captain of *The Elizabeth*, a four-masted schooner

commissioned to take immigrants from England to Australia during the 1852 Gold Rush. As for Ernest Hall, his mother's father, we know he 'felt like he was entering Paradise' when, aged fourteen, he left London and caught his first glimpse of the Iowa plains and the Little Maquetoka River. Hemingway would always feel the same delight in nature, the sheer joy of drawing a deep breath of country air.

Pioneers must search for new horizons. Through his writing Hemingway left his mark on Paris, Spain, Italy and the mountains and plains of Africa. His own country was less transfigured except perhaps, Key West, the United States' southernmost outpost in the Caribbean. Nonetheless, he was always an American writer, indeed for many of his countrymen *the* American writer, whose directness and passion made him the embodiment of American life. Proud, courageous and forthright, a passionate lover of open spaces and freedom, he once said: 'I've read somewhere that my heroes are neurotic. But people forget that life in this world of ours is dirty. We usually think of a man as neurotic when things go badly for him. The bull is neurotic when he's in the arena, whereas he's sane in the fields. That's all.'

He also used to say that life was too short to waste one's time and talent. He called life 'grace under pressure'. That was his style.

Life is like a baseball field and 'we play in a league in which we neither ask for a handicap nor give one'. It's a tough league, but the ball is the same for everyone. The pitches may vary, but all of them can be used for the championship trials. Excuses and arguments are pointless. The only thing is to get on with the game.

When Hemingway was young, he would laugh at those unlucky people who tried to hide their baldness with long strands of carefully arranged hair or by wearing a hat. By the time he was 50, he had dropped this subject.

CHAPTER THREE

THERE MUST ALWAYS BE A WOMAN AROUND

WHEN ALL SHALL BE DESTROYED

AND IF NOT ONE, IT WILL BE

ANOTHER

Ernest Hemingway and his third wife, Martha Gellhorn. A morose
atmosphere on board the Tin Kid, the Pilar's *auxiliary boat.*

Martha Gellhorn, photographed in London by Lee Miller. Hemingway kept
this photograph of Martha at Finca Vigía. Their relationship was often fraught
because Hemingway could never accept the fact that Martha's writing career
was as important to her as he was.

On board the Pilar*, off the north coast of Cuba. Husband and fourth wife settling down for a siesta.*

The scar on Mary's cheek was the result of a car crash when their Lincoln skidded on the Calzada de Mantilla near Finca Vigía, during the summer of 1945. Hemingway was cut on the forehead, but the surgeon hid the scar between his wrinkles.

'Don't care nothing for the prospects. But suppose will brighten up as get closer. It has always worked that way. Am not very bright right now and Know I always soften up away from battle or is it bottle and get wonderful ideas about wanting to live, write, have a double bed and have our good fine life that we have ahead of us.' This was Hemingway writing to Mary Welsh on 8 November 1944. It was his first letter from the front to her, scrawled out with a blunt pencil on the coarse, light blue notepaper provided by the US Army. Hard-boiled as he was, a tough and solitary man on the war front who had written a book called *Men Without Women*, he already had three broken marriages behind him and there was almost nothing about married life that he didn't know, so he chose – as he always had – a 'wait and see' approach. But that lack of enthusiasm in the early part of the letter soon gave way to a more lyrical tone that was unusual for him.

He tells her that he loves her and the only way he can qualify that simple statement is to say that he loves her more and more as times goes by. Without her he feels 'just empty, sick, lonely' as if 'half of me were gone, more than half'. And he urges her to be 'patient and brave and good' in the tests their love will meet in the world. Wryly acknowledging this lapse into romanticism he defends himself with the claim that one of their 'loveliest adventures' has been trying to understand each other in a deep and caring way and not simply indulging their passion in 'loving and quarrelling, you know the sort of thing "I love you you're a slut. But ah God how I love you" school of loving.' In a wonderful metaphor he likens their understanding to concrete 'reinforced with the good iron bars of (their) love'.

And then his mood shifts again, and he promises that moments of such high solemnity will be rare. He will be 'as gay as gay can be' although that gaiety will conceal his desire to serve her as 'some very dull people' want to serve their country or their god. Indeed she is for him 'a very small god with a face that breaks my heart every time I see it and the lovely body with the jolly big behind'. And why does he feel this way? Because 'together we make us – and us is much better than either of us separately'.

They had met in London at the end of May 1944. Both were war correspondents – Mary Welsh was writing for the *Time/Life/Fortune* corporation, Hemingway for *Collier's*. Author Irwin Shaw, who had known Hemingway in the late thirties, was having an affair with Mary when he introduced them to each other during a dinner at the White Tower restaurant, only a few days before the Allied landing. 'I liked him right away,' Mary Welsh later recalled. 'I thought him great fun. But I can't say it was love at first sight.' And yet, within only a week, Hemingway had made up his mind to ask Mary to marry him.

In the presence of friends, he offered himself up to her in marriage like a sacrificial lamb. Mary thought he was joking, but Hemingway was not the sort of man to take no for an answer. He persisted and finally got his way.

On 19 November 1944, he was writing again to Mary from the front, a letter which brimmed over with a keen nostalgia for that idyllic 'somewhere', that haven where he longed to find himself with the woman he loved. It was not so much the real house he owned at Finca Vigía as a safe refuge from the dangers of the world and the risk of death, and the letter reads more like a father's bedtime story, familiar images woven into a fantasy to soothe and quieten a restless child. He pictures them meeting at Rancho Boyeros airport as she comes off the plane from Miami and their drive through the countryside to the place where they are to begin their new life. Naturally she will be anxious but there will be nothing to fear because even if everything else in the world is destroyed, his house Finca Vigía will have survived unchanged: it will be like a command post 'to write and work in amid desolation' and their purpose is, after all, to 'write and not simply live in perfect conditions'.

At the time, Cuba seemed infinitely far-removed from the war that was still raging in Europe: he could dream that the remote island over 3700 miles away would always be spared the death and destruction both he and Mary had witnessed in France and Germany. Little did he imagine that the Bay of Pigs landing and the missile crisis of 1962 would bring the Cuban anti-aircraft artillery right into the garden of Finca Vigía. Only seventeen years after the end of the Second World War, the world escaped nuclear confrontation by a hair's breadth, and Cuba was less than ever in its entire history a Garden of Eden sheltered from world events.

Hemingway joined Mary in Paris during the first week of December 1944. But on the 17th, hearing of Von Runstedt's last great offensive, he left Mary to join Buck Lanham and the 22nd Regiment of the Fourth Infantry Division at Rodenbourg, despite the fact that he had 'flu.

It was at Rodenbourg that Ernie, known as 'Captain Illiterate', 'Kraut Hunter' and 'Ole Doctor Hemingstein' by his army buddies, had to wage another battle, a strictly personal one in which he had to use all his strategic reserves to break out of encirclement. It was time to call an end to his long-standing commitment to his third wife, Martha Gellhorn, a love which had sickened and declined, but which was not yet dead.

Martha's counter-attack took place on Christmas Eve. She arrived at the 22nd command post on a surprise visit. Hemingway's friend Colonel Ruggles had gone to a lot of trouble on his behalf, sending a jeep to Luxembourg to fetch Martha – 'to do Hemingway a favour', he explained, 'but I'm afraid I rather put my foot in it'. Her behaviour was aggressive and she seemed determined to wreck Hemingway's new found happiness with Mary, but he was patient and kind because it was Christmas. Martha relied too much on her beauty (as the Germans had on their tanks); in the end, she had to acknowledge the obvious truth that her husband was in love with someone else. Everybody at Rodenbourg was exhausted by the time she left, but at least the matter had been cleared up between the two of them.

Over the years Hemingway said such horrible things about Martha that no one quite believed him. His assessment of her was based on a deep-rooted misogyny that owed more to Latin *machismo* than to accepted Anglo-Saxon attitudes. His theories about women can be summarized as follows.

Women make great friends but lousy enemies. They go completely crazy every 28 days, but can be delightful when they want to be. A man must always remain on his guard, as women are the only bipeds who will go on boxing even after the gong. 'Maybe the female kangaroo does too. I wouldn't know.'

Women need to feel jealous of something. If a woman has no real reason for jealousy and the man she lives with happens to like his work, she'll be jealous of that. If he's a writer, she'll be jealous of his books. But the moment the man manages to convince her that he'll earn enough through his writing to buy her a mink coat, she'll start loving his work for its own sake and not just because it brings in money.

In spite of what women subject men to on their account, a woman believes that a man has to keep *his* word right to the end. If the man has mentioned a 'mink coat', she'll never let him forget it. She'll forget everything else she's been given, but that one thing will remain forever etched on her memory. And she'll get it out of him in the end. Of course, a man must never breathe a word against a woman's family; on the other hand, he has to agree without question with her own criticisms. The least disobedience in either respect will cause havoc.

Hemingway once said that he would like to write a story about a whore; the only problem was that it was impossible ever to find a woman who admitted to being

A bear hug for Mary after a successful day's pigeon shooting. The photograph is taken at the Cerro Hunting Club.

Previous page: At the Cerro Hunting Club in Havana. Hemingway tells a few hunting and fishing anecdotes to anyone who will listen.

There is much dispute about who this mystery woman in white is. Hemingway's physician, Dr José Luis Herrera Sotolongo, is adamant that she is Pauline Pfeiffer, Hemingway's second wife, who occasionally visited Hemingway at Finca Vigía. Other Hemingway cronies insist that she is Mary's mother. She is actually Mary's cousin Bea, Mrs Homer Guck.

one. Most women go to a great deal of trouble proving they're not whores. If the man goes along with that, his women will put up with him; if he's a writer, they may even condescend to like what he writes.

But unless they're abnormal, women attach far more importance to sex than to writing. They have a fifth sense when it comes to guessing whether a man is a good screw, just as a hunting-dog senses the presence of game. Not one of them is capable of appreciating a man's talent as a writer, except for one, 'whose name begins with M. Shit,' Hemingway concluded. That final word is added in Hemingway's own handwriting to a typewritten fragment found at Finca Vigía. But did the 'M' refer to Martha or to Mary? Both of them were writers after all.

Hemingway seemed to believe he had found the ideal woman in Mary. At last it would be possible to lead the perfect existence, a life in which both of them would be, as he wrote to her on 20 November 1944: kind and never ruthless, except with those who tried to make them waste their time and their lives. Mary would have to teach him how to be '*polite and* ruthless' on the phone with callers who disturbed him.

In the same letter he recalled Mary asking him what they would drink in the morning when they were in the

A trip with Mary to the Valle de Vinales, in the extreme west of Cuba, in 1951. Hemingway is wearing the guyabera, *a shirt with breast pockets popular with Cubans.*

Bermudas – the sort of intimate question that would be bound to crop up in a relationship with a man like Hemingway – and he suddenly recalled that he owned seven cases of pre-war Gordon's Gin, probably the last remaining bottles in the world. Unhesitatingly he offered her this treasure. In his opinion gin was not the ideal night drink but she could have it 'for anything else (I can make lovely Martinis) and have Noelly Prat too.'

In the morning, if there was no Perrier-Jouet available, Scotch was best. 'Do you like Scotch with good Soda without ice? Very good. Also Whisky and lime and soda to make Whisky sour.' There was no point in worrying about what they would drink at night because their days would be so full they would be too 'happy and tired and fine feeling' by the evening for serious drinking.

The life he wanted them to lead was a simple one: to get up in the morning and eat a breakfast of two eggs 'any style' with good fried ham or Canadian bacón, a glass of tomato, orange or grapefruit juice, and some papayas and mangoes, attractively presented on a tray. He would ring once for his own breakfast to be brought to him, twice for Mary's, and three times for the two breakfasts together.

Mary would be able to sleep as long as she liked, and he would sometimes have finished his day's work by the time she woke up so they would be able to spend the rest of the day enjoying themselves. But if he still had some writing to do, she could do whatever she liked. She could read and loaf about at the pool, and 'let everything in you thats been tired come back slow and strong and good (me too) – and you may not be bored at all – just maybe happy

the way we always were when you didn't have work'. If they felt like hearing some good music for a change, they would listen to their Capehart record player and they could buy any recordings she wanted at the Liberty Music Shop in New York.

In many ways it must have been an intoxicating affair: the celebrated author, offering an idyllic retreat from the horrors of war. Finally she agreed to marry him. They were each divorced from their respective spouses, married on 14 March 1946 and began their life together at Finca Vigía. But then, in September 1948, they decided to go to Italy. It was their first trip to Europe since the Second World War and they sailed to Genoa. Hemingway saw Fossalta – the place where he had been seriously wounded in 1918 – and then, in December, he was invited to shoot on the estate of Count Carlo Kechler. It was there, in Latisana on the River Tagliamento, that he met a beautiful but penniless young countess called Adriana Ivancich. He later described their meeting in *Across the River and Into the Trees*; there is a scene in which a certain Colonel Cantwell goes hunting and meets a girl called Renata. Hemingway's description of an ageing man falling in love with a very young woman is extremely close to his own experience, except that Colonel Richard Cantwell does not have a Mary Welsh waiting for him back home.

Hemingway invited Adriana to visit him in Cuba, and she turned up for a three-month visit one day in the autumn of 1950 with her mother Dora. Her brother, Gianfranco, an aspiring writer, had arrived in Havana the previous November and soon became a *habitué* of Finca Vigía (living in the tower for three years) and one of Hemingway's circle.

Adriana's arrival triggered off a succession of epic battles between Hemingway and Mary. It was a very bad period for the author as well as for his wife. His personal doctor, Dr José Luis Herrera Sotolongo, has described the situation: 'Ernesto had started drinking and could no longer do any writing. A rotten time for him... On one occasion I had to interfere bodily. I left the house at four in the morning when I saw the danger was over. They had threatened each other with firearms, and each of them had a shotgun. I had to take their guns away and hide them in my car. I took them back to my house. This was in the Batista days and [carrying guns] was extremely risky. That night I wrote to tell him that our friendship was over, but he called me the next day and asked me to help him dry out, as he had decided to stop drinking.'

But Adriana was not the only cause of dispute between them. On Saturday, 1 June 1953, the Hemingways were skirmishing again. Mary's first words to him that morning were:

'You stick your nose into everything. You get furious the moment someone prints a line about some country you've been to. For example, that guy who wrote a book on Spain.'
    'Which guy?'
    'That Frenchman.'
    'Oh, Malraux? Malraux's OK, but who else?'
    'Dos Passos on Michigan. It drove you crazy.'

They got angrier and angrier and went on arguing for the rest of the day over some complicated business matter involving a contract and Alfred Rice, the lawyer who had taken over Hemingway's affairs after the death of Maurice Speiser in 1952. They also fought over Bill Lowe, editor-in-chief of *Look* magazine, who had made Hemingway several offers for a series of articles on his private life. Mary claimed that Ernest hadn't told her about Lowe's proposal, but he maintained that, on the contrary, they had discussed the matter at great length. He added that he had two witnesses to the event: Leland Hayward, the co-producer of the movie of *The Old Man and the Sea*, and his wife, Nancy. The Haywards had been staying with them at the Finca at the time, and the four of them had discussed the offers.

'On the same day, she called me every name in the book and insulted me throughout lunch over some laundry business,' Hemingway complained. 'I left the table and when I came back she screamed so loudly that the servants and Taylor – who's stone deaf – all heard her.'

This particular war had been declared a few days

before, on the opening day of an annual marlin fishing contest. Because he had lingered too long at the Floridita bar, Hemingway had to put up with Mary's virulent scolding and nagging in the car and, later on, at home, in front of guests. Exhausted by the interminable argument as well as by the day's fishing, he went to bed early that evening.

Towards 1.30 am he was awakened by Mary's tearful reproaches and was unable to stop her. He usually put up no resistance in such circumstances, and was content to wait until the storm had abated. For a moment he was tempted to say to Mary: 'I'm a little hard of hearing. Are you thanking me for the little yellow convertible I gave you?' But he controlled himself and decided instead to go and sleep on an armchair in the living-room. He did not return to the bedroom until 5.00 am, knowing that Mary would be asleep by then. He got up again at 6.00, made himself breakfast and sandwiches for the day, and slipped out of the house before she woke up. He went to his boat and greeted everyone cheerfully without mentioning what had happened.

That Friday, at lunchtime, he once again had to endure Mary's loud nagging on some futile pretext. He pretended to ignore it and was thus able to enjoy a pleasant evening and a good night's sleep, in spite of the tropical storm that raged outside. He got up at 5.00 am on Saturday morning to check that the house and garden had not suffered too badly during the hurricane. When he opened the mail later, there was a letter questioning the existence of the *Look* contract, and this was what sparked off the all-day fight with Mary.

By Sunday evening, at the end of the marlin fishing contest, Mary's temper had improved. A few days later, Hemingway jotted down the following: 'Mary (after a double and a single martini): "What can I do to help you, darling?"'

The storm really was over. But these drawn-out battles drained Hemingway, particularly as they recurred at regular intervals, though a couple of months could go by without trouble. He admitted that Mary's reproaches were sometimes justified but he couldn't accept the fact that they were heaped upon him in public or in the middle of the night. He hated his wife's screams, her terrible insults and unfair accusations when she was in a bad temper. They wrecked his peace of mind and prevented him from writing.

Hemingway believed he went out of his way to avoid arousing Mary's jealousy over other women, and he did his best to be punctual at mealtimes. He also tried hard to be kind to her, rushing to answer the phone so that it wouldn't wake her if it rang in the morning. Surely it wasn't his fault if she heard it before he did? He gave her

Hemingway would often say of himself that he was an old lion, ready for action. He is pictured here with Adriana Ivancich, his latest 'prey', whom he met near Fossalta del Piave in Italy in December 1948. The real lion in the photograph met Hemingway on the plains of Africa in 1934.

Hemingway with Adriana Ivancich, the model for Renata in Across the River and Into the Trees. *In the novel, she is a naive young girl in post-war Italy who seduces Colonel Cantwell of the US Army. In real life, she was a penniless countess who introduced a new note of marital discord between Hemingway and Mary.*

At the Cerro Hunting Club. In Africa, Hemingway learned to shoot with one hand, in case of emergency. Here, he sees no danger, and relaxes, his defences lowered to all potential threats.

presents. Perhaps, after all, Mary was just a nagger, like his previous wives. He would have to shed his final illusions concerning women and retreat into a shell of indifference. But he was reluctant to give up something which he placed extremely high on his scale of values: love between husband and wife. For the time being, his house was quiet. Hemingway and his wife could go off to Cayo Paraíso to celebrate their reconciliation.

Cayo Paraíso – Paradise Key – was the name Hemingway gave to the location better known as Mégano de Casigua, which lies about 180 miles from Havana, approximately 5 miles off La Mulata Bay. The writer would go there when he wanted complete seclusion to work, with no visitors and no telephone calls to distract him. He followed the same daily routine as at Finca Vigía: getting up early, writing until eleven o'clock, then off to swim, fish or sail, exploring the coastline with Mary, half-naked and free, just as he had dreamed in a letter to her dated 18 November 1944.

In an extremely evocative mixture of memory and

imagination he describes the 'dark blue, almost purple' of the Gulf Stream with its crossing eddies in the current, their view from the bridge as the boat follows the flying fish up into the rocky coves and their anchorage, behind the barrier reef at Paraíso with the sound of the sea and the motion of the tide pull to lull them. And that first drink of the evening as they lie with their legs touching sipping 'a tall coconut water, lime and gin' and watching the 'lovely blue miniature mountains'. And he says 'Pickle, do you like very much? . . . and you say whatever you say and then there is that night and the next day is another day and in the morning we can sleep as late as late as ever . . .'

The only major disadvantage of Cayo Paraíso was the difficulty of getting hold of enough ice – an extremely important point for Hemingway, who had a great thirst and a passionate addiction to Creole cocktails, particularly daiquiris. His friends in Havana, Dr Herrera especially, helped him to solve the problem; on Sundays, they would fill the boot of the doctor's Chrysler with great blocks of ice and drive down the coast to La Mulata harbour.

*An impromptu
photograph at the stern of
the* Pilar.

*The sheepish look of an
overly attentive host. His
solicitude for the comfort
of a nubile young
American guest, during a
sailing trip, may have got
him into trouble.*

Hemingway would be waiting there for them, his beard fuller and his tales taller than ever.

Hemingway and Mary spent a lot of time at Paraíso in the late forties and throughout the fifties. Though they led a pleasant and relaxed existence there, Hemingway grew ever more despondent, bitter and dissatisfied with life and with women each time he returned to Finca Vigía. The notes he jotted down over this period which have remained at the house give some idea of his mood: 'If I had known then that each time we went out to dinner in Havana she'd throw her glass of wine in my face, and that one day I'd worked hard, she...'

Or again: 'Any woman prefers to dig her grave with her teeth rather than to work for a living with her hands.'

Hemingway loved a lot of women in his life; perhaps none more than Mary, who was with him right up to the end. She had come to Havana looking for happiness, love and fame. Only she, Hemingway – and God – know what she actually found there.

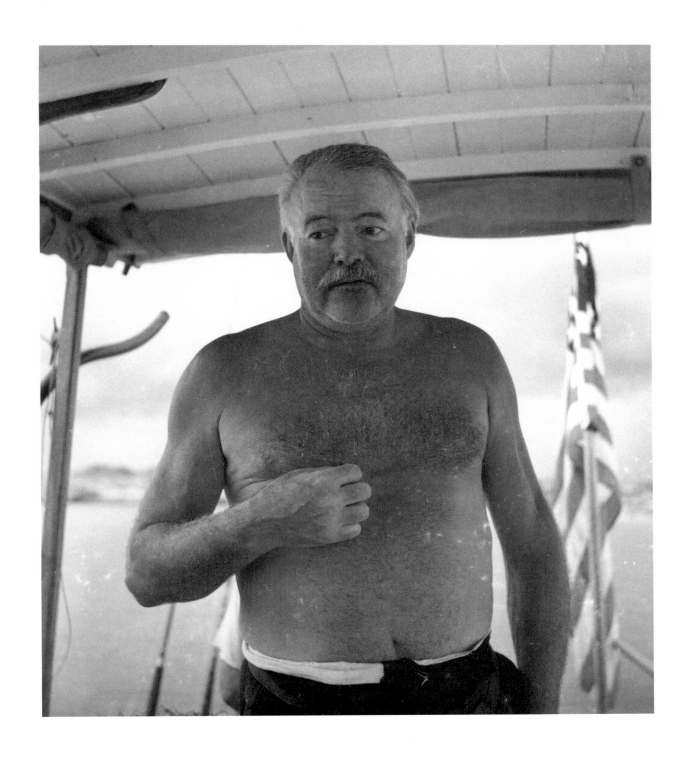

CHAPTER FOUR

ON BOARD THE PILAR, HEMINGWAY

PUTS OUT TO SEA ONCE MORE

ON THE BLUE WATER

FISHING, LAUGHING, DRINKING AND

FISHING AGAIN

*On the terrace of a café at Cojímar: with Anselmo Hernández
and Gregorio Fuentes, skipper of Hemingway's boat, the Pilar. Hernández was
one of the fishermen on whom the writer based Santiago,
hero of the* The Old Man and the Sea.

*The annual Hemingway marlin-fishing competition took place for the first
time in 1950. It is said that Hemingway had to be asked many times before he
agreed to let this competition, which was organized by yachting and fishing
clubs, carry his name. He saw it as an ill omen: 'A lousy posthumous tribute to a
lousy living writer.' In the foreground is Gregorio Fuentes, at the bow of the
Pilar, and in front of him some of the yachts lined up across the channel to the
bay of Havana before the start of the second competition.*

With Adriana,
1950–1, on the flying
bridge of the Pilar.

That day there were no fish. They had caught nothing all day. Irritation turned to anger as Hemingway became convinced that it was his companion's fault: poet Archibald MacLeish was scaring away all the fish. Finally he proposed a characteristic solution. They would land on one of the nearby keys and have a good fist-fight. That would make everything all right again.

With his 'well-known, enigmatic hyena's smile' – the expression was Hemingway's own – he landed MacLeish on one of the tiny islands between Boca Grande and Snipe Keys. By now MacLeish was furious with Hemingway too and he was delighted to get off the wretched boat. But there was to be no fight; a few moments later, the boat sailed away, disappearing over the horizon.

MacLeish walked up and down the deserted beach for hour after hour. There was plenty of time to recall one of

his best-known poems, in which he had compared Hemingway to 'a sleepy panther'. In the end, he owed his rescue to Pauline.

Nothing much could surprise Pauline Pfeiffer, Hemingway's second wife, any more, but she was startled all the same to see Ernie return to their Key West home without his great friend Archie. He sat down on the porch and casually started opening a few bottles of beer. Only when Pauline questioned him did he admit to having abandoned Archie to his fate. Pauline had never been able to accept that cruel, unscrupulous side of 'Wild Ernie'. She told him in no uncertain terms what she thought of his conduct and forced him to fetch his stranded friend. Just as the sun was sinking below the horizon MacLeish was rescued. The poet earned a nickname from that adventure: henceforth he was known as 'the Robinson Crusoe of American poetry'. Even Hemingway would call him that on the quiet evenings they spent together on the porch of the Key West house when the inevitable breach between them had healed.

Only a fisherman can hope to understand Hemingway's reaction on that particular occasion in the summer of 1936. His pride was wounded and this must explain his otherwise unaccountable behaviour. Every fisherman who ever lived has experienced that feeling of injured pride when the fish just aren't there. In Hemingway the feeling took on colossal proportions.

It was during the Depression of 1929–33 that Hemingway first heard about big-game fishing in the Gulf Stream. Not that his informant, Joe Russell, was particularly interested in fishing. But he had smuggled many a precious cargo of rum and other illegal beverages from Cuba to the Keys: these were still the Prohibition years and many good Americans had been 'driven to despair' just like Russell. The booze went straight to his bar, Sloppy Joe's on Green Street, off Duval, in Key West.

Russell had gone to live down on the southernmost tip of the United States long before Hemingway and Pauline moved there. He had played a minor role in the heyday of the gang-wars, when Jim Colosino and Al Capone's men were fighting over the sector. An independent, he was tough and shrewd enough to retire in the nick of time, hanging onto his most precious belongings: his boat (the *Anita*) and his bar.

He was just the sort of character Hemingway loved. Russell's name appeared in one of the writer's 1933 sports articles for *Esquire*, though no mention was made, of course, of the more compromising side of his activities. Russell later served as a model for Harry Morgan, the larger-than-life hero of *To Have and Have Not*. There is a description in the novel of Sloppy Joe's and of a boat which is a dead ringer for the *Anita*. In Howard Hawks's movie of the book, Humphrey Bogart played Harry

Morgan and Lauren Bacall was his wife, Marie. The screenplay was written by William Faulkner, who took a lot of liberties with the book, but, although the film was shot in Martinique, it manages to evoke the atmosphere of Sloppy Joe's pretty well.

When Hemingway moved to Key West in 1928, he got into the habit of spending the odd hour at Russell's place 'just to down a few beers' and have a chat.

'Ernest,' Russell asked him one evening, 'do you know where you get the greatest fishing in the world? And the most enormous fish? Right here, m'boy. Right here.'

That was enough for Hemingway. He instantly chartered the *Anita*, a weather-beaten boat, 34-foot long with a 100 hp Kermath motor that never went faster than eight knots. Gregorio Fuentes, who was later to be skipper on Hemingway's own boat, the *Pilar*, called the *Anita*, 'a good rider', by which he meant that she offered little resistance to wind and wave.

On that first trip, in 1932, Hemingway and Russell crossed the *Corriente del Golfo* (or Gulf Stream) and went fishing along the coast of Cuba, beyond Havana. They stopped off at Cojímar, Mariel and Bahia Blanca, all of them well-sheltered harbours that served as good bases for their operations. They bought hooks from local fishermen and listened to their advice. Those fellows knew everything there was to know about the sea and its big fish.

They left at dawn every day, and stopped fishing around four or five o'clock in the afternoon. They would dock at one of the harbours along the coast and work out tactics for the evening: the plan was a simple one – to empty every liquor-shop and every distillery in Cuba. 'Josie' or 'Grunts' Russell, as he was called, did the talking for once, while Hemingway listened and the *Anita* gently rolled from side to side, its headlights making soft swaying patterns in the peaceful waters of the Cuban evening.

If Joe stopped talking for a moment, Hemingway

With Gregorio Fuentes and Mary. The flying bridge was the only modification that Hemingway allowed himself on the Pilar. It offered a clearer view of fishing operations. Sadly for Hemingway, the fifties saw a decline in the fishing along the Gulf Stream.

The Pilar *off the coast of Havana. Built in 1934 in a Brooklyn shipyard, she sailed the waters of the Gulf Stream without a break until 1960. Pilar is also the name Hemingway gave the gypsy in* For Whom the Bell Tolls.

would fill the intermission with an announcement: 'Still listening. Ernie here. Ernie talking to Mr Russell. Over.' The only microphone they used on such occasions was, of course, a bottle of rum.

During their excursions, Russell found it easy to convince Hemingway that smuggling was an adventure rather than a criminal activity. Years later, Hemingway admitted to Gregorio Fuentes that he had organized three illegal crossings with Russell, getting contraband rum over to Florida. On one occasion they sold their cargo for a hefty profit in a quiet mangrove swamp, and Hemingway earned enough that day to pay for half the expenses of his first safari to Africa.

Once Hemingway had discovered big-game fishing it became his abiding passion, and a recurrent theme in his later writings. Jackie Key, a famous fishing-boat captain, described how Hemingway 'spends the whole day fishing, then goes to bed fully dressed and gets up at dawn to start fishing again.' He learned quickly and soon acquired a formidable reputation.

Hemingway caught his first really big fish in 1933: a 468-pound marlin, which he managed to pull in within 65 minutes. It was a catch to be proud of, a complete and unqualified success, which he owed to his strength alone. He had refused all the special apparatus that might have made it easier.

His technique of struggling with his prey and pulling it in as quickly as possible so that the sharks could not take bites out of it made him an overnight celebrity in fishing

circles. By 1935 he had landed the biggest sailfish ever caught up to that time in the Atlantic; it weighed 119 pounds. That same year, near the tropical island of Bimini, 45 miles east of Miami in the British West Indies, he caught a 786-pound shark after an epic half-hour struggle. Both records were duly registered. To complete that triumphant year, he won every fishing contest organized in the Key West – Bimini – Havana triangle, outdoing even such famous champions as Lerner, Farrington and Shelvin.

But his new passion also led to some memorable fights to defend his name as a fisherman. One day, at Bimini, in 1935, the millionaire publisher Joseph Knapp dared to express doubts concerning the authenticity of Hemingway's descriptions of his maritime adventures as printed in *Esquire*.

Knapp was drunk at the time and as he sat on the jetty his attacks grew more insulting by the minute. Hemingway ignored him at first but once he had called Ernie a 'slob' and a 'son of a bitch', the writer replied succinctly – with two left hooks, followed by a succession of hamfisted blows that sent Knapp flying, face down, to the ground.

For several years afterwards Bimini's calypso singers celebrated this exploit in every bar on the island. Hemingway described the event in fictional form in his posthumously published novel *Islands in the Stream*. What he omitted to mention, however, was that he broke his own code of honour that day: never strike a man when he's drunk.

Cojímar, 1950. Ernest Hemingway, a talented fisherman.

Of course it was unthinkable for any self-respecting fisherman to practise his sport on a boat that did not belong to him. And so Hemingway began to dream of becoming a boat-owner. That dream came true in 1934 after a trip to Europe, when he got an advance of $3,000 from *Esquire* against future articles.

He was involved in the design of the boat, and then had it built according to specifications at the Wheeler shipyard in New York. It was sent down to Miami by train, and, though Hemingway usually despised tradition, he dutifully baptized it with a bottle of champagne.

The *Pilar* was a solid craft. Measuring 42 feet from bow to stern, it had twin engines and could go 500 miles without refuelling. It was a legendary boat in Gulf circles almost from the start, and Hemingway spread its legend further through his writings. It is one of the most famous boats in American literature.

The living quarters were a sanctuary reserved only for the happy few. They consisted of three separate compart-

ments under the fore-deck. One cabin contained two double berths with built-in drawers beneath the lower bunk, two closets and a small table. The second compartment contained a kitchen and washroom. The third compartment contained another double berth and two open shelves that were under the exclusive command of Gregorio Fuentes: this area was known as 'the Ethylic Department' because it was stocked with bottles of the hard stuff.

Just behind the helm were four dials; two indicated the oil level and the temperature of the engines, the other two were a tachometer and an ammeter. To the left, there was a board with vertical switches for the anchor light, running lights, bilge pump, wiper and search light. Gregorio was in complete control here. It was vital work because changes of speed determined the tension on the line when a big fish was hooked and thus the chances of landing it.

A marlin is hooked and the struggle begins. Hemingway estimates its weight is 300 pounds. The battle will last for two, perhaps three, hours. He is on top form and, at the helm, Gregorio is in complete command. Only Mary seems anxious. When the fight is over, one last task awaits Gregorio: hoisting the catch aboard.

The boat could comfortably hold seven people, nine at a pinch. It could carry 300 gallons of petrol and 150 gallons of drinking water in its reservoirs. It could carry a further 200 gallons of water in drums and demijohns and 2400 pounds of ice.

During 25 years of navigation in the Gulf, the *Pilar* proved to be an excellent craft, easy to handle and always steady, even when it was being pulled this way and that by a gigantic fish. It would even serve as a warship – a Q-boat, Hemingway called it. For many months it patrolled the Gulf in search of enemy submarines without ever suffering damage. Nor was it damaged by the great yearly fishing contests and other unofficial competitions organized by Hemingway. Three Hemingway wives were unable to introduce any changes into its garish decoration. Nor did the frequent 360-mile jaunts from Havana to Paradise Key in search of a little peace to write prove too much for the gallant *Pilar*. It remained 'truly a most noble vessel', as Gregorio Fuentes put it: big and stable,

with all its wooden parts made of fine dark walnut.

But years of fishing expeditions in the Mexican Gulf took their toll on Hemingway's skin. Over the years he grew more sensible and two of his more celebrated 'props' protected him somewhat from the sun: a tennis player's eyeshade and a thick beard. The beard became an integral part of his image; he had always hated shaving anyway. A tough guy is not supposed to have a sensitive complexion; in fact, it is assumed he has a tougher hide than most. Hemingway's complexion was delicate, whether he liked it or not.

It wasn't his fault that he was born in Oak Park, Illinois, a middle-class suburb of Chicago, where people don't need the leathery skin which he so envied his fishing cronies in the Gulf. That kind of skin withstands not only the harsh rays of the sun but also the salt air and the fishing line as it rubs harshly across your shoulders, arms, or hands, depending on the position you adopt to pull in your prey.

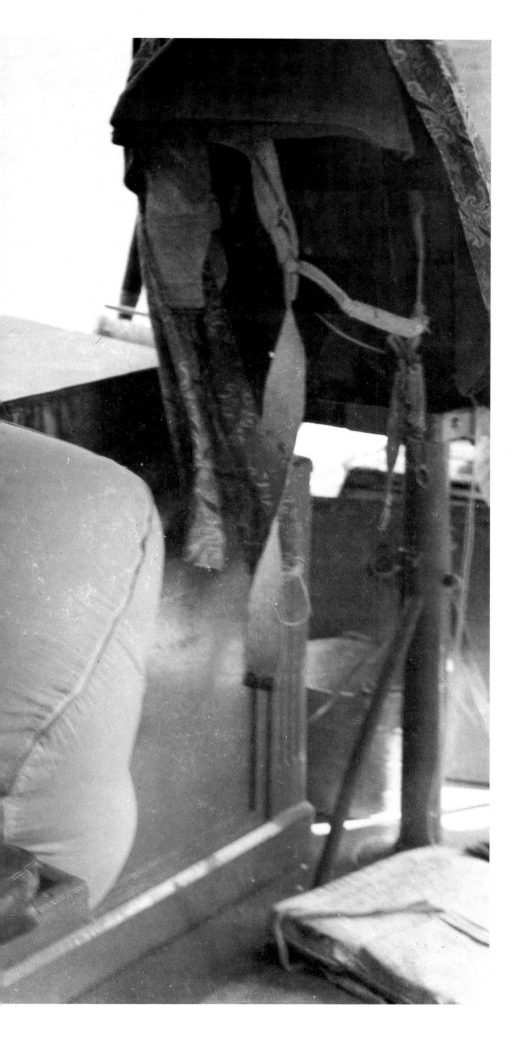

In *The Old Man and the Sea* Santiago, the hero of the novel, has a benign form of skin cancer. Hemingway claimed to suffer from the same ailment because the skin on his forehead and nose peeled constantly. During the 1954 fishing season, he got into the habit of making grandiloquent monologues to all and sundry, in which the subject of skin cancer recurred frequently.

'How do you like it, gentlemen?' he would call out when he was in a good mood. 'Here's old Ernie, that goddamned illiterate bastard who's beginning to do things in a revoltingly elegant style!'

He would stand at the helm of the *Pilar*, as steady as a rock, delighted to be wearing the sloppy clothes that were his favourite uniform when he set out for his 'sea-battles'. But he stood upright as ever and seemed taller than his actual height: 5 foot 11 inches. A vigorous, healthy-looking man with thick calves and shapely ankles, slender hips, square shoulders, a bull-like neck, and 17-inch biceps, no less. He had started putting on weight, especially around his stomach; and no longer wore a bathing-suit, preferring long, floppy bermuda shorts. In 1954 he managed to slim down to 229 pounds through constant exercise, and he hoped to reduce down to 192 pounds, which he considered the ideal weight for his size and build.

He was no longer in the habit of marooning his friends on desert islands. Fishing had ceased to be just a game or a pastime for him: it had become an art, and he had become a master in the art of catching spearfish in the *Corriente*. No wonder he made it the subject of *The Old Man and the Sea*, the novel which earned him the Nobel Prize for Literature.

In view of the time (midday), the temperature of 30°C, and the Caribbean sun, Rioja is not the ideal drink. But then Dr Herrera is not on board the Pilar.

Mary enjoyed life aboard the Pilar. *She had been around boats since childhood, loved the sea and adapted well to the Cuban climate.*

Every activity connected with big-game fishing was looked upon as a ritual and had to be carried out according to strict rules. And God protect anyone who dared break those rules from Hemingway's wrath! If you wanted to be in the small number of the elect who took part in the sacred rite, you did exactly as he told you or else...

The photographer Roberto Herrera Sotolongo tried on one occasion to prove that he had the skills required to become a champion of the noble sport. 'The rising star of big-game fishing' thus found himself one day with a rod in his hands, the line stretched to the utmost and quivering with ever-increasing violence. He had obviously hooked a big marlin which had been unable to resist the juicy bait cunningly prepared by Gregorio Fuentes, who truly deserved his nickname 'Grigorin the Wise'.

The marlin was hooked but had not yet quite registered the fact. Gradually, as it tried and failed to slip off the hook, it began to panic. Judging by the sporadic tugging and the tension on the line, Hemingway estimated it was a 300-pounder at the very least. The Ashaway n° 39 line attached to the tackle could easily withstand such a weight without snapping, and it held out against the fierce tugs at the far end, although the fish's strength was truly incredible. It was also obviously a smart fish for it began to concentrate all its efforts on trying to break the line rather than leaping out of the water in an attempt to slip off the hook.

Hemingway decreed that 'the implacable swordfish killer', as he had just christened Roberto, should be left to draw in the huge fish all by himself. A moment later the line lashed across the surface of the water like a gigantic silver snake. Roberto let out a long moan of agony as he toiled away like a true martyr to be deemed worthy of the

role Hemingway had so ironically bestowed upon him. 'The unbeaten revelation of the year in this man's sport' sweated and suffered, alternately scarlet-faced and ash pale, while Hemingway continued to vaunt his manliness, for all the world like a radio broadcaster commentating at a boxing-match.

Roberto's arms and torso began to look as stiff and elongated as the fishing rod he was hanging onto. Finally he dared to admit in an anguished whisper that 'his hands were getting a bit blistered'. But the marlin continued to fight for its life. Hemingway asked Roberto if it was day or night and did he see things in the sky that looked like stars or the sun? Roberto replied that he could see both suns *and* stars.

'Gentlemen,' Hemingway declared to his pals aboard, 'our Guru of the Depths is beginning to feel tired.'

According to Gregorio, there were three other people on board that day: 'sharpshooters' in the *Pilar* jargon, in other words 'plenty-big drinkers' known across every bar in Havana.

'Bob the Natural – the greatest sea-roamer since Jesus Christ' continued trying to draw in his catch, but a clumsy movement on his part released the brake on the ratchet of the reel. By this time he was so dazed that he could hardly hear Hemingway's ironic praise of his technique. All Roberto later recalled was that he himself was screaming at the 'f ... fish' to stop pulling so hard.

The only one who could still save the situation was the helmsman of the *Pilar*. Grigorin the Wise slowed down and, with his usual dexterity, turned the wheel left and right, following the direction in which the marlin twisted and turned. He also varied the speed so that the line remained just taut enough to tire out the fish, yet not so tightly stretched that it would snap. But one last, great jerk

on the line put an end to the duel. With a sound like a whiplash, the line snapped at last.

'There are some things one does well or else not at all,' Hemingway declared sententiously. 'If one isn't sure one can do them properly, it's better to give up the fight before it starts.'

Then, in much quieter, less jocular tone, he turned to his other cronies and asked them to say nothing about the incident. A pal had suffered defeat, and the shame of it need not be proclaimed far and wide.

Roberto got the message: in future, he would do well to stick to his favourite hobby, photography. Hemingway was not blaming him for his defeat, but for having involved himself in a trial of strength unprepared. As a result, there was a wounded fish somewhere in the *Corriente*, needlessly suffering, with a great steel hook embedded in its mouth. Its bleeding wound would soon attract droves of sharks, and it would die a horrible death.

Roberto went off to recover on one of the bunks, where he could sulk in peace with a delicious cold daiquiri. His brother, José Luis Herrera, Sinsky and Don Andrés remained on deck with Hemingway. José Luis Herrera Sotolongo was Hemingway's doctor and had been the medical commander of the Spanish Republican Army in 1937. Sinsky or 'Sinbad the Sailor' was Juan Duñabeitia, a Basque who commanded a cargo ship from Cuba to the States. Don Andrés Untzaín was a Spanish Republican priest, forced to go into exile in Cuba after the Spanish Civil War.

These three men made up the hard core of Hemingway's 'crew'. They were shrewd enough never to try and establish a record or claim that they were champions of any sort. They were not even remotely interested in big-game fishing and would never have made the same mistake as Roberto, for whom Hemingway coined yet another nickname: 'Bobby, the Happy Eunuch'. Their only goal was to get dead drunk on the *Pilar*'s plentiful reserves of rum, a task to which they had dedicated all their attention since the boat left the dock of the Havana Internacional Club.

José Luis Herrera was the only doctor who had the nerve to stand up to Hemingway and to challenge his pseudo-scientific theories about the effect of the sun's rays on the tender skin of Mid-Western intellectuals. Sitting in the *Pilar* with a glass in his hand, he would pronounce his diagnosis. 'Stop giving me that bullshit about your skin cancer, Ernesto,' he would say. 'You have a mild case of melanosis and nothing else. And will you please stop scratching at your peeling nose like that with your dirty fingers!'

Pauline Pfeiffer was the first of Hemingway's women to go aboard the *Pilar*. That was back in the days of the fishing contests and the trips to Bimini and Havana, the days of the drunken revels with the poets and publishers who came down from New York to visit Ernie, and who considered themselves lucky if they did not end up stranded on desert islands.

The Martha Gellhorn years coincided with the Second World War. Martha therefore spent many an hour gazing at the sea and at her husband as he fulfilled what he considered to be his patriotic duty. He was utterly absorbed by the task of submarine-watching, which he described as 'a rather different sort of fishing to the type I usually go in for'. He had stuffed the *Pilar* with machine guns and cases of hand-grenades and recruited 'the most efficient suicide crew ever to be found' to patrol the seas with him in the hunt for German submarines.

When he married Mary Welsh, his fourth wife, he was the unchallenged champion of American letters and of big-game fishing. But there were fewer pleasure-fishing craft about in the Gulf than in the pre-war years. He also tried to teach his last great love, the young Adriana Ivancich, the joys of fishing and preparing tackle during her visit to Cuba in the autumn of 1950, while attempting to resolve problems of a more personal nature, what José Luis Herrera dismissed as 'Ernesto's sentimental complications'.

One November day in 1954 Hemingway stood at nine o'clock in the morning on the pier of the Havana Internacional Club, on the western side of the bay. He had got out of his Buick station-wagon at the far end of the pier, giving his chauffeur, Juan, instructions that would keep him busy until three o'clock, when the *Pilar* was scheduled to return. He had no intention of doing any writing that day. He was going fishing, and he could afford to take a day off: he had been awarded the Nobel Prize. With him were Mary together with a few friends. A reporter from *Time* magazine who had managed to inveigle himself into the writer's good graces had been invited along too. Hemingway was wearing his usual old blue-and-white checked shirt, khaki bermuda shorts and the *Gott mit uns* belt he had removed from a dead German soldier on the Western Front in 1944.

He took stock of the inventory. He had heard the weather forecast over the radio in the Buick: it was going to be a hot day. Carefully he checked the beer and tequila reserves – the favoured beverages aboard the *Pilar* at the time, though they would soon be supplanted by Bloody Marys. Gregorio Fuentes, the ever-efficient skipper, listened to the weather forecast with him once again, and they were ready to leave. Hemingway took off his shoes and socks and hopped onto the boat with surprising dexterity. Standing at the helm, he steered the boat while

Off the north coast of Cuba.

that the waters are quite different in nature and temperature. Twenty generations of fishermen before Hemingway called the demarcation line between the two blues the *hilero*. He was as obsessed by the *hilero* as he was by the city of Paris or by the slopes of Mount Kilimanjaro in Africa.

Hemingway knew all the good spots for fishing, the places where he would have the best chance to catch the biggest fish. He had studied the movement of the *Corriente*. He knew that it originates to the southwest of Cuba, off Cape San Antonio and then follows the northern coast of the island, after which it flows up past Key West, Miami and Cape Hatteras, before turning in a north easterly direction towards Europe and the Canary Islands. Another current, known as the North Equatorial Current, then sweeps down, past the Canaries and crosses the Atlantic again towards the Caribbean and Yucatan to complete an enormous circle. Hemingway also learned that the Gulf Stream flowed nearest to Havana in an easterly direction, that it was 60 miles wide at that particular point, and that its speed depended on its depth, varying between 1.2 and 2.4 knots off Havana.

He knew the migratory habits of the spearfish and their feeding habits. It is to the *hilero* that the really big fish come to feed. If you open the stomach of a marlin to examine the contents, you will find every variety of small fish that lives just on the edge of the *Corriente*. The spearfish migrate from west to east, but are easier to catch when swimming in the opposite direction, just outside the *Corriente*, when they venture in search of food. Blue marlin arrive from April to May in this zone, but it is only from September onwards that you can catch the really big ones, the 'heavyweights', as Ernesto called them. The gigantic fish caught by Santiago in *The Old Man and the Sea* is a September fish.

Now in November, Gregorio had begun to get four lines ready: two of them were attached to the outriggers, poles on either side of the boat that are long enough for the lines tied to them never to become entangled. They are equipped with a special pulley system that starts to hum as soon as a fish is hooked.

Hemingway and Gregorio agreed to start fishing in the Cojímar area, 5 miles east of Havana. Gregorio took the helm and Hemingway went down onto the covered deck to read the papers and have his first drink of the day: tequila with lemon and ice. Without removing his cap, he lay down on the old, plastic-covered mattress; but these moments of pure pleasure were short. At 9.35 am exactly he heard the outrigger on the port side making the familiar humming noise as the line began to vibrate furiously. This was immediately followed by Gregorio's familiar cry: 'Feesh, Papa. Feesh!' To hell with the papers!

The *Time* reporter had been listening to Hemingway's

Two distinguished members of Hemingway's regular 'crew': Gregorio Fuentes, the skipper, lighting a cigarette, and José Luis Herrera Sotolongo, the doctor, dozing.

Gregorio raised anchor.

The *Pilar* chugged past El Morro, the fort at the entrance to Havana's harbour, and people waved to 'Mister Way' from the jetty built across the reefs of the narrow harbour entrance. The landmark gently receded into the distance as the boat set off once more to sea. It was still warm at this season. The engines purred contentedly, even though they were going at full speed. A shoal of silvery sailfish already surrounded the vessel, clearly visible even in the polluted waters of the bay.

The *Corriente* flows only 325 yards off El Morro, and you can easily distinguish the current. The surface of the Gulf Stream is a much deeper blue than the water that lies on either side. It is that contrasting colour which indicates

theories about Marcel Proust; according to Papa, no writer had ever been more thoroughly familiar with the milieu he sought to describe. But Gregorio called out again, even more stridently 'Feesh! Papa! Feesh!' And Hemingway instantly forgot about Proust and hurled himself on his rod. The *Time* man realized that his readers would not learn much more about Hemingway's opinions on the French writer that day.

On another, almost identical occasion, later that month, Gregorio caught sight of some really big fish. Hemingway grabbed his reel and was soon trying to pull in his prey, slowly, carefully, without undue hurry. The whole art of bringing in a fish is not to leave the line too slack so that it can wriggle off the hook. But you must not pull too hard on the line either, or else it might snap. Hemingway started winding in the line; in such circumstances, he looked as large and firm, his drawn-in stomach as flat and hard, as in his youth... Gently, gracefully, with supreme elegance, he smoothly drew in the line, releasing it slightly from time to time, and then pulling on it again. To avoid putting too much strain on his back, he used mainly his arm muscles and rested his whole weight on his right leg. At regular intervals, Gregorio would turn to glance at his boss, to see how stretched the line was, before returning to his steering.

Hemingway identified the fish he had hooked simply from the tension on his line and from the weight.

'A tuna,' he called out to Gregorio. 'A fine tuna!'

Calculating his strength, he drew the fish nearer and nearer the boat. The line was growing shorter and tighter every second. Soon enough, a tuna was thrashing about on the deck of the *Pilar*, its scales shining like copper and silver in the sun.

'Great!' Hemingway said. 'A fish on board before 10 o'clock is a good sign. A very good sign!'

A couple of dolphins appeared near the bow. Their entire bodies emerged from the water. They seemed happy and full of trust, not in the least frightened by the *Pilar* and its occupants. Hemingway gazed at them. His unbuttoned shirt flapped in the warm breeze. The mid-morning light cast his patriarchal shadow onto the wet planks of the deck.

'Dolphins,' he said. 'Aren't they superb?'

The Cojímar fishermen who fish along the whole coast of Cuba remember him well. They still refer to him as *El Viejo* or Papa. That is the image of himself that he left there: an old man on his boat, his skin burnt by the sun, with a white beard and a tennis eye-shade.

Those fishermen say he smelled like all old men: occasionally of soap and toilet water, at times of medicine,

On the beach at Cojímar: the end of a day's fishing. The fishermen's children are delighted by 'Mister Way's' success.

*A great catch. This marlin
weighs more than 350
pounds, and it struggled
for half a day.*

and often, very often, of rum. But he was also tough as
nails. He could spend a whole day struggling with a fish,
resisting the constant jerks of a creature that sometimes
weighed 500–600 pounds.

Hemingway called the fishermen 'the Sons of Death'.
They liked that name. It transformed their daily toil into
an epic, something that Papa alone had perceived it to be.

When *El Viejo* caught sight of a modest fishing craft
along the Cojímar coast, he would steer the *Pilar* in its
direction and ask how the Sons of Death were doing. How
work was getting along? Was the *captura* good so far?
Then he offered the Sons of Death a drink, which they
never refused. Their respective boats gently swaying side
by side, they would continue chatting for a while.

Today, the man with the long bermuda shorts and the
thick beard, who stood with legs wide apart, holding his
fishing rod, at the stern of his boat, is still a legendary
figure across the *Corriente*. If you decide to go there one

day with your old Tycoon bamboo fishing-rod and you tie
a line to the outriggers in the waters of the Gulf, you may
run into him. His boat is made of stout walnut. You will
recognize the outriggers on either side. Its Chrysler
motors chug along almost noiselessly. It sits wide and low
on the water and is heading for the East Cape at the same
speed as the *Corriente*.

But, to be worthy of that vision, you will have had to
put up a great fight with your rod and your reel, without
cheating, using your own strength and endurance alone.
What counts is the fight, however wearisome it grows.
Never mind if it lasts from morning till night, pushing you
to the limits of your strength. Only when you have won
that battle with yourself will you perhaps catch a glimpse
of Papa, standing boldly and watchfully on deck, wearing
the eye-shade, his blue-checked cotton shirt and his khaki
bermuda shorts, sailing forever on the dark blue water of
the *Corriente*.

The international fishing club in Havana harbour, 1954. Hemingway visited the club regularly, and anchored the Pilar there during the fifties. The club served as an operational base during the Hemingway marlin-fishing competitions. The two fish shown here were caught by Gregorio Fuentes, the skipper of the Pilar. The peto weighed 82 pounds, an *extraordinary weight for this species. The white marlin is a fairly average size, but its steadfast courage earned it a place in the photograph. Hemingway, in a sailor's sweater, had just returned from his second African safari and was still suffering from the effects of his plane crash.*

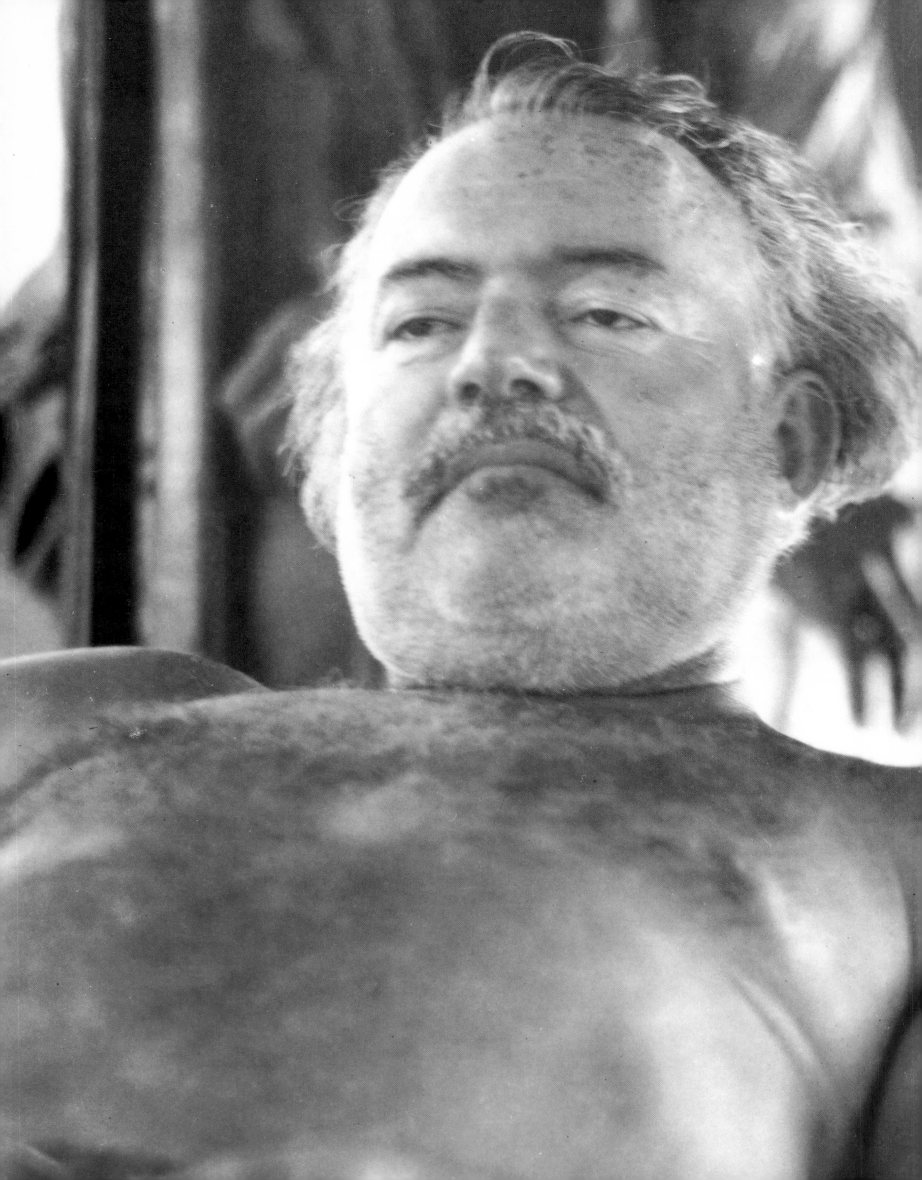

CHAPTER FIVE

THE NECESSARY, SELF-IMPOSED ASCENT TOWARDS

NGÀJE NGÀI – THE HOUSE OF GOD

BELIEF AND RITUAL IN THE PURSUIT OF

IMMORTALITY

*Since early childhood, Hemingway had loved hunting. Cuba offered few
opportunities for the devoted sportsman so he had to content himself with the
occasional shot at a passing gull or the more structured pleasures of pigeon-
shooting at the Cerro Hunting Club. Mary took up the sport, and in 1956
Hemingway described her as 'a fair wing shot'.*

On the shooting range at the Hunting Club. The Remington and the eyeshade are preserved at Finca Vigía.

Hemingway killed himself in a log cabin, in Ketchum, Idaho, on Sunday 2 July 1961. The writers of obituaries for the press, recalling the false announcements that had followed his second plane accident in Africa in January 1954, waited for confirmation of his death. When it came, his family, especially Mary, his wife, insisted on behaving as if this was yet another in the long line of accidents which had chequered his life: he had died cleaning his 12-gauge Boss shotgun.

And yet the facts can leave little room for doubt. There was no instrument in the cabin that Hemingway could have been using to clean his weapon, and a man accustomed to handling firearms since his childhood would never have made the mistake of cleaning a loaded gun.

Hemingway used to say to his friends at Finca Vigía that he would much prefer to kill himself than let Death – 'that old whore' – decide for him when his time was up. He had worked out the method he would use; sometimes he would rehearse it in the presence of Dr Herrera. Sitting bare-foot in an armchair, he would rest the butt of his Mannlicher Schoenauer .256 on the living-room rug, lean over to press the two barrels against the roof of his mouth and push down on the trigger with the big toe of his right foot until there was a click. Then he would raise his head with a pleased smile on his face.

'This is the technique of hara-kiri with a gun,' he would tell Herrera Sotolongo, who was far from delighted with these 'suicide-training' sessions and spent them sipping a glass of vintage Rioja from Hemingway's wine-cellar. 'You see, kid,' Ernesto would add, 'the palate is the softest part of the head. Remember that, old chap. It might come in handy some day.'

Hemingway loved firearms and he loved hunting, especially big-game hunting. Roberto Herrera took photographs of him, standing at the helm of the *Pilar*, holding a small-calibre shotgun, on the lookout for sea-birds. He considered it good target practice, and a fine way of not growing rusty. He also belonged to the Cerro Hunting Club near Finca Vigía. There was an arsenal of different guns in his house: big-calibre shotguns, rifles, pistols, and at least 50 trophies and animal skins to show for his skill as a hunter. Hemingway used to tell his third son, Gregory, that he would have liked to earn his living just shooting a charging rhinoceros or an enraged bull-elephant. The big cats were more of a problem: they vanished in a flash and you often missed them. The best thing, really, was to steer clear of them.

He sometimes described his travels in Africa and how he had explored the Chulu mountain area, where no white woman had ever been seen before. It was there in early 1954 that Mary tried, for 37 consecutive days, to bag a lion. 'The day that Miss Mary shot her lion was a beautiful day. That was all that was beautiful about it,' he wrote. But in his opinion she had deserved her lion, and the lion should have been proud to be killed by a lady as gutsy as Miss Mary.

Mary was an erratic shot: she could kill a small kudu deer with a single bullet through the throat at a distance of 375 yards, but she was also capable of missing 'Jesus Christ sitting on William Faulkner's lap, even with the light at her back'. She would shoot anything that moved and she loved it, but her small size was a handicap. Both she and her gun-porter were so tiny that animals weren't afraid of them. The shyest of creatures would amble up to them, and zebras would bare their teeth at her. But at least she had the satisfaction of appearing in one of Hemingway's best and most amusing essays on Africa, 'The Christmas Gift'.

Guests at Finca Vigía were often struck by the sheer number of African amulets and ritual objects scattered about the house.

Mary would say, 'They're just souvenirs.' But Lucia Castillo Cabrera, the wife of Juan, the chauffeur, was sure they had more significance: 'The Americano was a *believer,...*' When a Cuban says this, it means that the person in question adheres to one of the many sects presided over by *santeros*, who are to be found throughout the island. Lucia remembers that, one day, Hemingway said to her husband:

'Juan, I've heard that your wife is ill and that nobody knows what's the matter with her. Is that true?'

Juan replied that his wife was indeed sick and the doctors couldn't figure out what was wrong with her.

'You must take her to see a *certain person*, Juan. I'll tell you who to go and see.'

It was a *santero* in San Francisco de Paula, near Finca Vigía. He prescribed a treatment which, among other things, consisted of dressing all in white, even down to one's shoes. It had cost a thousand pesos, which was a big sum in those days. Hemingway paid for everything and told Juan: 'She saw the one she needed to see. She did what she had to do.'

To this day Lucia wonders how her husband's employer had learned about the existence of the *santeros* and why his house was so full of amulets, why he wrote with his bare feet resting on a small kudu hide, and why he seemed so attached to the ceiba tree which grew in his garden.

Hemingway often said that he would like to be buried at the foot of that tree, between its roots. He thought it would make a fine grave, without any tombstone or epitaph. Just him and the tree.

It so happens that the ceiba – or silk-cotton tree – is regarded as sacred by the Afro-Cuban cults. Whoever chops it down, cuts off its branches or mutilates it in any way can expect disaster to befall him. Hemingway had a deep respect for his tree.

On one occasion, a root of his ceiba began to extend under the house, doubtless in search of water. Though it had started to raise the floor tiles in the guest or Venetian room, Hemingway categorically refused to let anyone touch the root. He claimed that it would grow in another direction when it found no water and that the floor tiles would fall back into place. As far as Lucia was concerned, 'The Americano knew what he was doing.' But Mary did not agree.

She waited until Hemingway had to go into Havana, and, as soon as he was gone, sent for a gardener she had hired especially for the purpose. The man took up the floor tiles, loosened the earth around the root, uncovered it and chopped it off, all under Mary's urgent instruction. When the task was completed, they both suddenly had the strange feeling that there was someone else in the room. They looked up and, aghast, realized that Hemingway was standing behind them, brandishing one of his double-barrelled 12-gauge Remingtons.

Mary remained frozen to the spot, but the gardener leapt out of the window, still holding onto the root. Hemingway raced after him into the garden, blasting his shotgun in the air.

The ceiba at Finca Vigía was reckoned to be at least 150 years old. In 1985 it threatened to cause such serious damage to the house that it was cut down and a young tree, only 5 feet tall, was planted in its place. Every single day, in her house at El Vedado, the aged Lucia says a prayer for the Americano: 'He was a good man. He knew what he was doing and why he did it.'

On one occasion he said to Doctor Herrera: 'You must pierce my ears. I must have it done before the child is born in Africa!'

According to Wakamba rites, a father must wear gold rings in his ears during the pregnancy if he wants his child

Hemingway found the mongrel Blackie wandering in a street near Finca Vigía. He became the house mascot and was trained as a pointer. Blackie was killed by the rifle butts of a patrol from Batista's army, which surrounded Finca Vigía in 1957.

to be born safely. During his second safari to Africa in 1953–4, Hemingway had 'married' a young Wakamba girl called Debba. Out of respect for the rites and fearing the gods, he wanted to wear rings in case a child was born of this union.

Hemingway returned from his first safari in 1935, and decorated his Key West house with his earliest trophies. He had not written anything much for the last five or six years and had set off for Africa a sad, embittered man. The trip gave him a new lease on life. He began to write once more: two great short stories which took Africa as their inspiration – 'The Snows of Kilimanjaro', and 'The Short Happy Life of Francis Macomber' – and *Green Hills of Africa*, an account of his African journey.

In 'The Snows of Kilimanjaro', a youngish writer leads a sterile existence with his rich wife. They set off on an expedition and the man falls ill. As he lies dying on a camp-bed, he recalls his past life and thinks of all the works he will leave unwritten. The story opens enigmatically with the following curious tale.

> *Kilimanjaro is a snow-covered mountain, 19,710 feet high, and is said to be the highest mountain in Africa. Its western summit is called by the Masai Ngàje Ngài, the House of God. Close to the western summit there is the dried and frozen carcass of a leopard. No one has explained what the leopard was seeking at that altitude.*

The leopard had lost its way. It died trying to reach the House of God, or immortality. Harry Street, the hero of 'The Snows of Kilimanjaro', never wakes up from his strange nightmare and dies, without having reached the Ngàje Ngài. But in February 1937 Hemingway set off for the Spanish Civil War, taking with him his old portable Royal typewriter. He returned from his final tour of duty in late November 1938 to write a masterpiece, *For Whom the Bell Tolls*.

For the moment the approach to the House of God was 'all-clear', to use one of his favourite combat-pilot expressions. But, like the leopard, Hemingway ultimately felt unable to complete his task.

Hemingway at the Cerro Hunting Club, around 1948. A bastion of Cuba's intellectual bourgeoisie, the club had its heyday in the forties, and was popular with some of the American magnates who lived on the island. Hemingway and his third son, Gregory, won several pigeon-shooting competitions there. In 1961, after the revolution, the club became a school for machine gunners and the militia.

CHAPTER SIX

HEMINGWAY AT LARGE

NO MAN IS AN ISLAND

CLUB AND BAR, CRITICS AND CAUSES,

AND THE CIRCUS

With the fishermen of Cojímar, during the filming of The Old Man and the Sea,
*1955. They helped look for the great fish required for filming and appeared as
extras. After Hemingway's death they erected a bronze bust of him in a plaza near
the shore, in memory of their friendship and of the prosperity he brought this
Cuban community.*

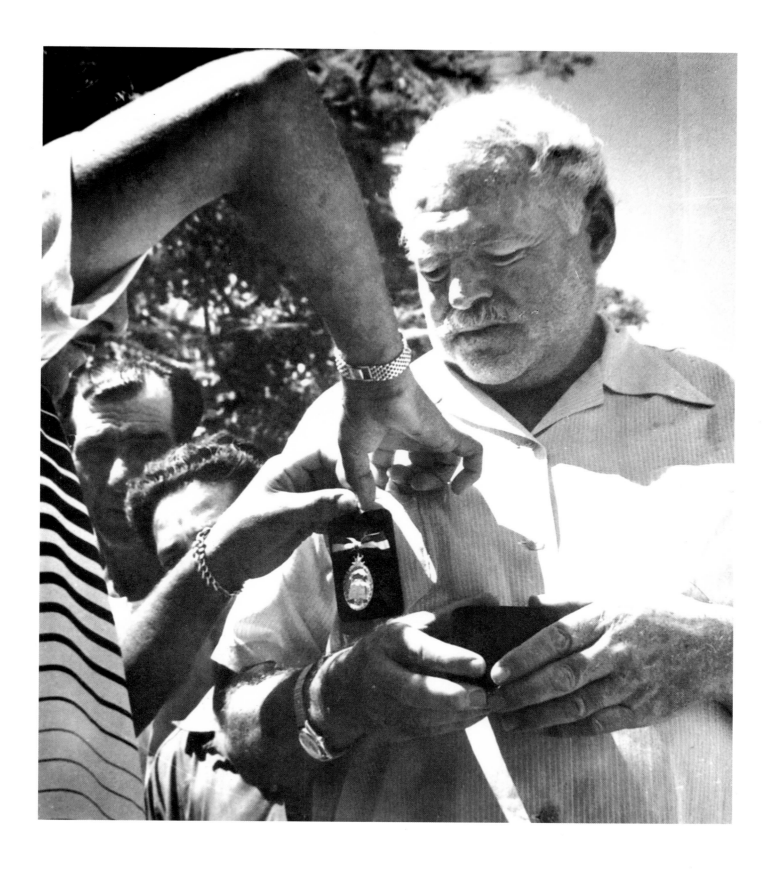

111

15 May 1960:
Hemingway's only
meeting with Fidel Castro.
The Cuban leader won
the individual
championship at the
Hemingway fishing
tournament. It is said that
he invited Hemingway to
fish trout in a lagoon near
the Bay of Pigs.

The Hunting Club was an important stopover in the Hemingway itinerary. It was located in the Cerro, the residential district of Havana where the Creole aristocracy lived. Hemingway first went to the club in the early forties. He would ask his friends to meet him there for picnics washed down with copious supplies of beer and interminable pigeon-shooting contests.

He was always relaxed, smiling and good-natured at the club, though something of a 'loudmouth' according to a few of the more formal members. He was never reluctant to pose for photographers, aiming at a pigeon with his Remington double-barrelled shotgun. Wearing a cap with an eyeshade and an expression of absolute concentration, he would pulverize pigeon after pigeon.

Apart from the occasional flight of ducks in winter, or a rare species of deer that was fast becoming extinct, the placid Cuban landscape offered Hemingway very little opportunity to practise one of his favourite sports. Sometimes, just to keep in shape, he would stand at the helm of the *Pilar* and take pot shots at sharks with his rifle.

Africa was a long way off: shooting at pigeons and sharks was almost the only hunting available in his adopted country.

Finca Vigía, the *Pilar* and the Hunting Club were all places where those who encountered him could expect to deal with Hemingway on his best behaviour: an affable, peaceful, straightforward sort of man. At the Floridita on Obispo Street he was completely different. He felt at home amid the noise and confusion of this thriving bar in the heart of Havana. He loved the place: it opened onto the street so he could get his fill of 'the free life of the city' as he downed his daiquiris. He grew less fond of it when air-conditioning was installed in 1947; walls had to be built to enclose the open space. Still, he got used to it in the end and resumed his old habit of perching on the high oak stool drawn up to the bar as complacently as on a throne. He would greet his friends enthusiastically and have long chats with some; short, mysterious exchanges with others. And he had his own way of getting rid of

*In 1953, the Ringling Bros and Barnum & Bailey
Circus came to Havana. Hemingway wrote
enthusiastically about its wonders, its quality, the
nobility of its animals, the skill of its acrobats and
the magnificence of the show. 'The circus is like
a dream,' he wrote in one of his notebooks.*

Hemingway acquired a special pass which allowed him to visit the circus animals and 'talk' to them.

bores and hangers-on.

Manuel Bell, otherwise known as Blacaman or El Blaca, one of his fishing friends, recalled how the two of them were drinking their tenth daiquiri together one evening when some American tourists came up to Hemingway to ask for his autograph. Hemingway granted their request quite amiably, then turned his back on them, rested his elbow on the counter once more and took up where he had left off. 'The artist is a solitary man,' he was explaining to El Blaca, 'and solitude is a part of his training. He learns to put up with it and to make the best of what it has to offer him...' Suddenly, one of the tourists grabbed him by the arm and asked for another autograph. Without bothering to get up, Hemingway dealt the fellow such a blow with his fist that it sent him reeling back ten paces until he crashed into the tables on the street outside.

Explosive reactions of this sort made Hemingway seem hardboiled, the epitome of the mean, pitiless tough guy. Any yet, though he boasted of having dispatched a whole platoon of German soldiers with his switch-knife during the Second World war, he adored animals. He loved cats and dogs (some claim there were as many as 57 cats living at Finca Vigía at one time) and looked after the frogs, lizards, iguanas and wounded birds that found their way into his garden. He refused to let his trees be cut down and hated the boys from San Francisco de Paula, the village nearby, who threw stones at the fruit trees.

He even kept a bat preserved in formalin like a precious relic. Some have claimed that he kept it because it reminded him of the bat on the Bacardi label, the best rum to be had in Cuba. This may be so, but it must be added to Hemingway's credit that the creature had flown into Finca Vigía one night and smashed its skull against the walls in its desperate search for an exit. Hemingway

tried to nurse it back to health with six drops of gin, a penicillin injection and a mixture of aspirin and mercurochrome on its skull, but to no avail. At dawn Hemingway was found holding the little creature he had christened Bad Bat as he tried to find the pulse under its right wing.

'Good old Bad Bat is dead,' he finally announced.

The bat was preserved as a tribute to its brave, silent fight against the pain and suffering it had endured.

When people asked Hemingway how he could reconcile his passion for hunting in Africa with his solicitude for the animals that lived at Finca Vigía, he would reply that Africa was like a war zone, whereas his house was a place of peace.

Going to the circus was another favourite pastime. The sheer beauty and skill of circus performances were 'a true-life, happy dream', one of the genuine pleasures of life that people could buy for a modest sum.

The Ringling Bros and Barnum & Bailey Circus came to Havana for the fifth time during the winter of 1952–3. It was headed by John Ringling North, known as 'the Northern Star', and his son Henry, who had taken over the day-to-day management of the circus upon his return from the Second World War. Under the leadership of these two men, the circus had reached a standard of excellence which seemed insurpassable. They were both determined that the circus should be a perfect miracle of organization and efficiency, offering the most complete, most dazzling performance each and every time. In other words, it really had to be 'the greatest show on earth'.

It was like a mobile city, with a population of 1500, its own hospital, fire-brigade, police force, legal-affairs service and advertising agency, as well as the inevitable repair workshops, hairdressers and beauty parlours. It comprised in all 43 tents, covering an area of fifteen acres,

*He seems to have discovered a strange affinity
with the brown bear. Copious photographs were
taken in the belief that Hemingway would write
an article about the circus.*

With the circus horses. Kid Mario, an ex-prize-fighter, says that Hemingway once performed with the Circus Miguelito. The owner advertised the event without any real agreement from Hemingway, who spent two hours with a pair of old lions, kitted out in his African hunter's outfit, and then demanded his fee: $10,000. The proprietor of the down-at-heel circus passed out from the shock. When he came to, Hemingway let him off, with a promise never to do such a thing again.

and the big top alone, with its three rings, could hold an audience of 16,000 people.

Hemingway went to see the show on New Year's Day, 1953. He was lucky enough to see Unus, the man who could support himself upright on one finger; Mroczowski, who could blow out a candle placed on the ground as he galloped past it on his white charger; Dieter Tasso, the tightrope-walker; and the lion tamers and trapeze artists. He was an ardent defender of those who earned a living as circus artists. 'Take Unus,' he used to say, 'a fine, intelligent man, a great guy who earns a living balancing himself on one finger while most people can't even stand properly on their own two feet.' But he also knew that such perfection could only be achieved at the cost of tremendous effort and suffering. Some of the men who worked in circuses might be mean bastards, but it was impossible to hate even a real son of a bitch when he walked across a tightrope miles above your head, performed an amazing triple somersault, or faced tigers and bears inside a cage.

Hemingway was less enthusiastic about clowns. 'They give as good as they get,' was all he would say. The two star clowns of the Ringling Circus were Otto Griebling and Emmet Kelly, who was known as Sadface. Hemingway once said of Kelly: 'How do you expect me to laugh at a guy called Sadface, who really looks sinister?'

As for the animals, he was as enthusiastic about them as if he had been taking aim with his Mannlicher somewhere out in the African bush. Leaning back against the bar of the Floridita, he would describe the impression they had made on him: the big cats leaping over their tamer's head as naturally as if they had been charging their prey, just like a lioness teaching her cubs to hunt. And then there was Jeannie! Doing her tricks with such extraordinary grace. If she'd been a male, she'd have made a great baseball short-stop. You have to be extreme-

ly fast to make a good short-stop, and Jeannie the elephant weighed at least three tons. Ringlings' young Indian elephants were incredibly smart: as smart as humans in many ways.

Legend has it that Hemingway promised the Ringlings he would write a piece on their circus. In return, they gave him a free pass to visit the animal quarters as much as he liked. He spent many hours wandering from cage to cage, talking with the big cats in a special language that no one understood, not even the tamers.

Hemingway enjoyed circus games, but word games were his passion. His publisher, Charles Scribner, told the Puerto-Rican film director, José García, the following anecdote.

Hemingway went into Scribner's New York office one morning and made a bet with him that he could write 'the shortest story in the world'. A genuine, full-length story with a proper plot in only six words. He would write it down on a slip of paper and if Scribner and the others present agreed that it worked as a short story they would each have to pay him $6.

'We all read it, and we had to pay up,' Scribner recalled. 'That story brought him $60'.

The story, without a title, read: 'For sale, baby shoes never worn.'

He might play with words, but he defended his books tooth and claw when they were under attack. Sometimes he went about it 'Hemingway-fashion', grabbing reviewers by the neck or the lapel and socking them in the face. Max Eastman discovered this to his chagrin after writing a critique for the June 1933 number of *New Republic* titled 'Bull in the Afternoon'. The title parodied Hemingway's *Death in the Afternoon*, the classic examination of bull fighting which had been published in September 1932. Eastman claimed that Hemingway's 'tough' style often sounded phoney; it was 'a literary style, you might say, of wearing false hair on the chest'. Hemingway took Eastman's comment as a personal insult to his virility.

The two men ran into each other in New York a few years later, on 11 August 1937, when Hemingway returned from the Spanish front to raise funds and sympathy for the Republican cause. The meeting took place in the office of Max Perkins, who edited Hemingway's books at Scribners. Hemingway arrived without phoning ahead to find piles of Eastman's *Art and the Life of Action*, containing a reprint of the hated article, lying on a table; Perkins and Eastman were planning a new edition of Eastman's *Enjoyment of Poetry*.

'What do you mean accusing me of impotence?' Hemingway growled.

Eastman replied that he had never written anything of the sort. He picked up a copy of his book and found the

With Gary Cooper at that legendary bar, the Floridita in Havana. The other people are typical of those described by Hemingway in a diary on 4 September 1956: aspiring writers, officials from the American Embassy, members of the Lyon's Club or the American Legion, FBI agents or characters who will be murdered within the next week or the next year.

piece. But Hemingway ignored the passage Eastman wanted him to look at and began reading out loud a section of another paragraph before tailing off into muttered curses. 'Read all of it, Ernest,' Eastman pressed him. 'You don't understand it ... Here, let Max read it.' Perkins began to read, but Ernest grabbed the book, saying, 'No. I am going to do the reading.' Then glaring at Eastman, he slammed the open book across his face so hard that Eastman collapsed, his nose almost broken by the heavy cardboard cover. Eastman later told journalists that his nose was in that condition because he'd had a fight with Hemingway and had grabbed him by the fuzz on his chest; the hairs, being false, had come away in his hand and he had toppled over onto his nose.

Hemingway also boasted of the exploit when he gave an interview to the press at the docks just before sailing back to Spain on the *Champlain*. 'The man didn't have a bit of fight. He just croaked, you know, at Max Perkins, "Who's calling on you, Ernest or me?" So I got out.'

Throughout his life Hemingway was ready to defend a worthwhile cause with great enthusiasm and warmth. He felt a strong sense of solidarity with the entire human race, and he practised what he preached concerning justice and courage. It is true that he loved a good fight, and that adventure, violence and firearms all played an important part in his life; but he did not rush indiscriminately to any war front just for the pleasure of wielding a

gun, going hungry and feeling cold. 'No man is an island unto himself.' Hemingway was a man amongst men. He sometimes made the wrong choice, but he had the courage to take sides because fundamentally he loved his fellow man. During the period March 1937 and November 1938 he made four journeys to Spain, then in the throes of bitter civil war, as a war correspondent. All the fighters in Madrid knew Hemingway by sight: a tall, powerfully-built man with a square jaw and a big smile, wearing a suede jacket, high hunting boots, a black beret and small, circular, steel-rimmed spectacles. When he went on his rounds in the Spanish capital, he carried a Magnum pistol, smuggled in past customs, as well as an explorer's knife and a gourd – a relic from the First World War – full of cognac. His pockets were crammed with raw onions and when he was hungry he would nibble on an onion, washing it down with a swig of cognac.

He seemed to lead a charmed existence, calmly strolling under the bombardments and effortlessly ducking bullets as he went over to soldiers to offer them a drink. The Dutch film director, Joris Ivens, who was filming the documentary *The Spanish Earth* in the same sector, was in despair at the sight of Hemingway, brought in as his consultant during the shooting and was 'running as many risks as the average infantry officer'.

The Spanish Earth was produced by Contemporary Historians, a production company created especially to

The Floridita, September 1955. The days spent filming The Old Man and the Sea *were marked by blazing sun, spray and sea breezes. The nights were gentler. Hemingway thought Tracy was bad casting for the gaunt Santiago but Tracy, who co-owned the film rights, got the part.*

fund and distribute this film and the earlier *Spain in Flames*. Its board of directors included Orson Welles and Lillian Hellman, who was also supposed to write the commentary. She went over to Paris, but fell ill there and was unable to join the film crew in Spain. Initially Hemingway, who had met Ivens in Paris in March 1937, gave organizational rather than artistic help, including invaluable advice on how to film the fighting on the Madrid front. But eventually he was asked to write the commentary too. Hellman, who was an experienced scriptwriter, declared after a showing of the film in the sixties: 'Ernest did a very good job of it.'

Orson Welles had originally been earmarked to read the commentary but Lillian Hellman and Fredric March disliked his rendering. In the end Hemingway had to record his own work. When the film was screened in Hollywood, Welles and Hemingway went to see it together. All Welles had to say to the writer was: 'The film is lousy and your voice is too high.' Hemingway wasn't the sort of person to take such an insult lying down. He threw himself on Welles and, by the time the two men had finished fighting, the screen and seven rows of seats needed repairing; as for the projectionist, who had tried to break up the fight, he had to go to the hospital to have stitches put in his scalp. Orson Welles later maintained that Hemingway had misunderstood him. In any case, Hemingway's reading is the longest recording we have of

his voice; it is a precious and moving document.

Hemingway had been wholeheartedly committed to the Spanish Republican cause from 1936 onwards. When he returned to the States in May 1937 for a brief fund-raising trip, he began to revise the near-completed manuscript of *To Have and Have Not*. As a result of the events he had just lived through, he altered his text, deleted one section and rewrote the speech Harry Morgan makes just before he dies of a bullet wound in the stomach, turning the words almost into a manifesto: 'A man. One man alone ain't got. No man alone now. No matter how a man alone ain't got no bloody fucking chance.'

The book was panned by reviewers, some referring to a new 'Stalinist' Hemingway and others dismissing its 'rudimentary protest' as well as its sentimentalism. They did not see it as an appeal to human solidarity, a tribute to one man's courage as he discovers the forces of darkness and blind hatred unleashed upon a people desperately fighting for its freedom, yet losing the battle in the end.

He loved the places where human beings congregate. It would be interesting to know how many hours he spent sitting in the Floridita. Today many people go there on a literary pilgrimage. They sit near his empty stool and ask for a daiquiri bitter no sugar and a double portion of rum, which was what Hemingway always ordered. It was the right drink in the right place for that sort of man.

CHAPTER SEVEN

THE MAN WHO COULD MAKE

EVERYDAY A FIESTA

BUT WHO PREFERRED COOL EVENINGS

WITH HIS CATS AND A GLASS OF WINE

*Finca Vigía, 1955. Spencer Tracy is still in town dress, a
sober contrast to the Hemingways' relaxed style.*

*Adriana Ivancich (right), Hemingway's last great love,
arrived in Cuba for a three-month visit late in 1950.
She and her mother stayed at Finca Vigia.*

The Cerro Hunting Club, 6 September 1950. Listening to the weather report from the National Observatory on his battery-powered Zenith, Hemingway seems preoccupied although Gregorio Fuentes is confident, as always. A tropical depression from Guadeloupe threatens Cuba, but this will not be the first time Gregorio has seen the Pilar *through a hurricane.*

Mary, Hemingway's widow, wrote a letter to her ex-chauffeur, Juan Pastor, on 4 July 1964, just three years after his death. In it she recalled with affection and nostalgia the pleasant existence she had led at Finca Vigía. Trapped in the sweltering heat of a New York summer she missed the cool, palm shades of Finca Vigía and the 'good life we led out there'. She reminded Juan of the time he found a bundle of money on the garage floor and took it straight to her. 'I can't tell you how proud I was of you for having acted the way you did.' Now, her chauffeur-driven days over, she was down to standing on street corners watching for a taxi. But it was not so much the inconvenience as the loss of camaraderie that she regretted: cabs being 'not as much fun as our rides into Havana with you at the wheel of the old Chevy, or was it another car?'

In fact, it was a Buick. The Hemingways also owned a Chrysler, which Juan took out only on special occasions.

But Juan was not just a chauffeur. Sometimes, after a really long session at the Floridita, he would have to lend a hand to get his boss safely back into the house.

One particular occasion, in January 1953, stuck in Juan's memory. He had managed to drag Hemingway out of the car and was helping him stagger up to the house. As they reached the front door, the kind-hearted Juan gulped and decided to say what he had been meaning to say for a long time: 'Don't take it badly, boss, but you drink too much. It's bad for you, boss. Everyone can see that. Liquor has side effects, but they're direct effects in your case.'

Hemingway tried to answer, but he could only mumble something that sounded like 'Whatsa matter?'

Juan took his chance, coming back quickly: 'Look at you, boss, you can't even talk straight. You can't even give a proper reply!'

An argument of sorts began. Hemingway's eyes were glazed and he could produce only a succession of angry grunts as Juan pointed out to him that on the journey home he had thrown up twice and even peed in his pants.

The early days of Finca Vigía. In this calm and peaceful place, Hemingway built an enclosure where he could admire the bloody beauty of a cock fight. Finca Vigía was equipped with a wine cellar, copses of areca palms and mango and coral trees, a swiming pool and a cock farm. René Villarreal, the young black servant, had plenty to do.

132

Idaho, Christmas 1947: a light-hearted family moment. The previous year his second son, Patrick, had suffered a serious illness. With the help of Pauline, his mother, Hemingway had nursed him devotedly for three months.

The Floridita bar. His
Havana refuge did not
free him entirely from his
social obligations. In
town, as at home, he had
to endure some great
ordeals: posing beside an
admirer or listening to an
after-dinner peroration.

Hemingway conveyed furiously that it was a Ringling
Circus tiger who had soiled his pants, not him. One point
led to another with a lot more grunting and mumbling on
Hemingway's part. Finally the two men grabbed hold of
one another and they were soon rolling about on the
ground. In fact, they began to roll, gently at first, still
intertwined, from the front door of the Finca towards the
main gate, past a clump of mango trees. By this time they
were both thoroughly exhausted, and Hemingway had
sobered up somewhat. He burst out laughing, threw his
arm around Juan's shoulders, gave him a bear hug, and
announced they must celebrate their reconciliation by
opening another bottle of rum.

The lights were always on at Finca Vigía. Sometimes
Hollywood film-stars lounged by the swimming pool,
drinking whisky; flamenco dancers and *toreros* sipped
vintage Cuban rum to the sound of music. This was the
gay, easy-going aspect of his life, where events always
ended in laughter, even minor family dramas like the tiger

incident. What Mary was to recall most vividly after his
death was the sheer excitement of living with someone
like Hemingway, surrounded by stars and high society,
with armies of faithful, hardworking local servants to cater
to their every need. It was this world that she obviously
missed so much on the stifling New York summer day of
1964, when she wrote her rather condescending letter to
Juan in Havana.

An all-the-year-round party? It was so dazzling, so
glamorous, so literary that it sounds like something out of
a B-movie. But sometimes the movie was more like a
slapstick comedy. Like the time Hemingway lay in wait for
his next-door enemy, the wealthy Frank Steinhart Jr, and
then hurled stink-bombs and firecrackers into his garden
just as he was giving a grand reception. There were also
the Sundays spent in illegal betting on baseball championship games, something Hemingway tolerated, even
though he was manager of the local San Francisco de
Paula team, Las Estrellas, in which his third son,

Gregory played.

On other days, especially in the forties, he would place bets on his fighting cocks. At one time he had as many as twenty birds at Finca Vigía; they were looked after by the gardener, José Herrero, whose nickname was Pilicho. A magnificent, white-tailed champion once earned him $800. When Hemingway made a will in 1956, he left his cocks to Pilicho, just as he gave his beloved *Pilar* to Gregorio Fuentes, his .22 calibre Winchester to René Villarreal, the young black house-servant, and the meadow adjoining Finca Vigía to Pedro Buscarón, a neighbour who had always been particularly helpful.

The image of Hemingway left to us by Dr José Luis Herrera Sotolongo is of a very simple man, a man quite different from the legendary Papa and the tales of never-ending fiesta. Herrera kept a record of all the evenings he spent at Finca Vigía between 1945 and 1960, the times when there were no foreign visitors about to disrupt the normal rhythms of life in the house. Through the doctor's eyes we see Finca Vigía and its floodlit garden from the inside.

Hemingway is reading a book, a magazine such as the *New Yorker*, or else *The New York Times*. He finishes off the bottle of wine left over from dinner while Mary and Herrera play canasta. Soon Hemingway grows sleepy. He leaves the empty wine-bottle by his armchair, says *buenas noches* and takes his leave before midnight. Shortly afterwards, the doctor drives back to his home in Havana.

Now the house is dark and silent. The servants have all gone home. It is time for Hemingway's night duty. With a .22-calibre pistol stuck in his belt, a stout stick in one hand, and his dog Blackie tagging along behind him, sniffing the ground for any tell-tale traces, he patrols his territory. Nothing to report. It's off to bed.

In the morning, after several hours of writing and a couple of Tom Collins', Hemingway's blissful peace would be shattered by the arrival of René Villarreal and the mail: letters and postcards from friends, bills, never ending business with publishers and film producers, and all the nuisance letters you get when you are successful and famous. He was always conducting a running battle with one reviewer or another; many of them seemed to relish tearing his work to pieces.

To protect himself from attacks of this sort, Hemingway wrote a preface to *A Moveable Feast*, the memoir of his life in Paris from 1921 to 1926, written during 1957–60 and published posthumously. 'For reasons sufficient to the writer,' he begins, 'many places, people, observations and impressions have been left out of this book.' Later he concludes, 'If the reader prefers, this book may be regarded as fiction. But there is always the chance that such a book of fiction may throw some light on what has been written as fact.' He was using a boxing technique to cover himself from the reviewers' body-blows: shield yourself with a left hook and let them have it with a right.

Hemingway wanted to live his life to the full: to travel

Perhaps this group wanted to capture for posterity the friendship that united them and the wonderful moments they had spent beside the swimming pool at Finca Vigía. One of them may have joked that the photograph would one day be published with the caption: 'Hemingway surrounded by unknown people'. He was not wrong.

'The boss loves me like a father.' Juan Pastor is
the Pedro of Islands in the Stream and
Hemingway is Thomas Hudson. In the novel,
Hudson says that Pedro is bone idle, a careless
driver and a son of a bitch. In real life,
Gianfranco Ivancich (left), Adriana's brother
who lived at Finca Vigía for three years, is a
witness to relations that could not be more filial.

A bar on the harbour in Havana. Hemingway's personal record, established at the Floridita, was 12 double daiquiris without sugar. The classic daiquiri was invented by a Spanish barman working at the Floridita and comprised of rum, lemon and sugar over crushed ice, plus a dash of maraschino. Hemingway's version became known as a 'daiquiri à la Papa'.

The Floridita was not the only bar Hemingway visited. Many of them followed the Spanish-style bodega, with a long wooden counter at right angles to the street, metal shutters that opened the place up to passers-by and high wooden stools which the customers mostly ignored, preferring to drink standing up, with one foot resting on the rail.

Gary Cooper and other, unidentified visitors to Finca Vigía. The Hemingways adopted an open-house policy for local friends, even offering a delightful setting for a wedding reception.

to get to know people, to meet his destiny head on. But he also needed to preserve his private world. He tried to solve the dilemma by dividing his life up into separate compartments and disguising some of those compartments very carefully. He would discourage potential biographers by asserting that the only valid book was the one which described every facet of a man's life, every moment and every act of his existence – obviously an impossible task. And yet he did reveal a great deal of himself in his writings.

His was an approach which has much in common with the television documentary-dramatists of the 1980s. He created fiction by using real-life characters and situations. It was an approach which he first began to develop in his earliest days as a feature writer for the *Kansas City Star*. His stories are drawn from real-life incidents in which he was an onlooker or a participant. They can be called fiction only because he modified the original events somewhat. They are condensed, heightened versions of the facts, a reworking of the raw material which contrives to reveal the essential truth of events.

We recognize Hemingway in the hero, Krebs, in 'Soldier's Home' and Frederic Henry, hero of his great novel about the First World War, *A Farewell to Arms*. It was he who was wounded in the leg, who was given those medals, and who went home, like his hero, disillusioned. He writes about himself again when he describes Santiago, the hero of *The Old Man and the Sea*, with the cracks in his hands from the fishing tackle and the 'benign skin cancer caused by the reverberating sunlight on tropical seas'. We know that this old man, who dreams of lions as he lies dying, is none other than Ernest Miller Hemingway. And the locations where the action takes place can easily be identified on a map of the Bimini coast and of western Cayo Romano.

In the novel *Islands in the Stream*, again published posthumously, many of the events of his own life are used, barely disguised, with considerable courage and honesty. Whereas in *A Moveable Feast*, which is more overtly autobiographical, he had taken great pains to portray himself as an attractive figure and to show off his best sides, in *Islands in the Stream*, the more fictional approach he adopts allows him to draw a self-portrait that has the truth of hindsight. It is written by a worn-out man, ten years older than he was at the time of the events described, now looking back on them with a disenchanted vision.

It was Malcolm Cowley, one of Hemingway's most faithful friends and among his most acute and sensitive critics who first broke the news, around 1949, that Hemingway had another major book in progress. He arrived back in New York from a visit to Finca Vigía announcing that Hemingway had a thousand pages, written in pencil, lying under a copper paperweight next to his portable Royal typewriter. The manuscript only needed a good title and a few revisions before it could be sent to a publisher. According to a well-established pattern, Hemingway would make an overall revision of his text once it had been typed out. 'And then,' Cowley claimed, 'when the veil is lifted, they'll discover that Hemingway has also written the greatest novel on the Second World War.'

He seems to have begun work on the project in 1946–7 and probably abandoned it in 1950–1. It was to be a vast undertaking, a war trilogy. The first section would deal with 'The Sea', the second and third with 'The Air' and 'The Land'. It was as though he wanted to outdo Marcel Proust, after having once announced his desire to 'knock Stendhal out on the ropes', and 'shoot down Tolstoy'. It would be a summing up of everything he had

Two of Hemingway's animals: at one time he had 57 cats, most of whom lived on the first floor of the tower at Finca Vigía. Hemingway was convinced that he had established a new breed by crossing Cuban cats with angoras. He was in the habit of giving them names containing the letter 's'. Thus Boise, Missouri and Spendi made an appearance.

At the Floridita bar in the fifties, with Colonel Charles Sweeny (second from the right). Sweeny was one of the few men Hemingway admired. A West Point pupil, he had fought alongside Madero in the Mexican Revolution, joined the French Foreign Legion, was a squadron leader in the RAF in 1940–41, and founder of the Eagle Squadron. Mary seems more occupied with Gianfranco Ivancich, and Roberto Herrera Sotolongo completes the group.

learned and experienced.

One fact *is* certain: Hemingway's flair as a journalist had not betrayed him. By the end of the Second World War, he had produced a wealth of first-rate material, and he had enough in reserve to write a novel as long as *War and Peace*. It would have been a great fresco of battles in the mid twentieth century.

'Hemingway could write a novel about the war on land, on sea and on air, based on his adventures alone,' Malcolm Cowley used to say. The part about the sea could be drawn from his wartime experiences aboard the *Pilar* between June 1942 and April 1944 as from time to time he patrolled the keys north of Cuba in search of German submarines, equipped by the intelligence agency with radio, machine guns, bombs and grenades. He could write about his many raids in the company of RAF pilots, including Peter Wykeham Barnes (later to take up Air Mar-

shal), both before and after D-Day. And, of course, he would be able to describe his wild jaunt, armed to the teeth and well-supplied with wine, vermouth and cognac, from Normandy to Paris with the 22nd Regiment of the US Fourth Infantry Division alongside his great hero and friend Colonel (later General) Charles Trueman 'Buck' Lanham; he could also narrate his experience in the Rambouillet campaign, during which he, together with an unofficial advance force of the Free French partisans, held the town for a day.

He would also have had to find a place for one really bizarre episode in his life. An old yellowing file dated 1942 found among Hemingway's papers at Finca Vigía contains a number of sheets of notes, carefully typed out on a Royal portable. The style is fluent and often elegant, the descriptions sometimes almost poetic. But at the same time they offer precise, extremely detailed information

A celebration for Spencer Tracy in a Havana night club, 1955. And another group shot in Hemingway's corner at the Floridita. Colonel Sweeny is third from the left.

The Floridita and another
celebration. Mary is
wearing a new black coat.
The handsome and
slightly uneasy man next
to her is none other than
Roberto Herrera,
Hemingway's private
secretary, on the other
side of the camera for a
moment.

*Juan Duñabeitía, known as Sinsky or Sinbad the
Sailor, was a captain in the Cuban merchant
navy. A frequent visitor at Finca Vigía, he
accepted without complaint the role of clown in
Hemingway's band of intimates.*

Sinsky was an enthusiastic innovator in his quest
for the perfect gin cocktail, but he never found
the right formula to relieve its after-effects on
himself or others.

The Cerro Hunting Club, around 1940. Hemingway is the guest of honour at a lunch to mark the publication of For Whom the Bell Tolls.

concerning the activities of the Nazis in Mexico.

They include a full description of a German pharmaceutical company called I. G. Farben, which served as a cover for agents of the Third Reich. There is also a report on the relationship between the German ambassador to Mexico and a group of right-wing intellectuals. One of these, a certain doctor, received money from the Germans to publish anti-Semitic literature. The report is full of anecdotes, sometimes amusing, with extracts from conversations and letters concerning the ambassador's attempts to set up and consolidate these contacts and to launch a full-scale propaganda campaign.

The same document also contains a study of Nazi activities in the coffee-growing area of Chiapas de Soconusco, where most of the haciendas were owned by Germans, obvious recruits for the Third Reich party. The zone is described as 'very remote and therefore of strategic importance'.

There is a coded signature at the bottom of the document. It is simply a number: A-39. In May 1942 Hemingway spent a week at the Plaza Hotel in Mexico and took advantage of his stay to do a bit of private investigating, as he could not yet join in the fray. The document in question is probably related to the undercover anti-Nazi undertaking, known as the Crook Factory, which Heming-

way organized in 1942–3.

In any case, there are eleven days in Hemingway's life which remain totally unaccounted for: at the end of April and the beginning of May 1942. The author's file at CIA headquarters in Washington has been expurgated; some of its pages cannot be consulted 'for reasons of national interest'. They would obviously contain useful information because most of them relate to the year 1942. However, it is impossible to guess whether those mysterious pages contain references to the writer's para-military activities or whether they betray a flirtation with Communism, as some have claimed.

Only a third of the trilogy was ever planned and written. As the title suggests, *Islands in the Stream* is the sea section. The hero, Thomas Hudson, is a famous painter. He is wealthy, proud of his tan and his great strength. He owns a house at Bimini and another in Cuba, as well as a boat 42-foot long. Hudson is a larger-than-life version of Hemingway, still strong and eager for adventure, still ready to go to war. All the places described actually exist. Hemingway first went fishing off the Bimini islands in 1935 and was still remembered as the American who drank straight from the bottle, a remorseless brawler who fought on the beach with Tom Heeney and took pot shots at the sharks that swarmed all along the coast. The

The Cabo Blanco Fishing
Club, Peru, April 1956.
The waters of Cojímar
proved uncooperative
during the filming of The
Old Man and the Sea and
a second unit had to go
south to the Pacific,
looking for an enormous
black marlin.

people were real too, even though their names have been changed. Leopoldina Rodriguez, a prostitute who worked the Floridita bar neighbourhood in the forties, has been renamed Honest Lil (Liliana La Honesta). Gregorio Fuentes is called Antonio in the novel, and Juan the chauffeur is called Pedro; but both men are described exactly as they were in real life.

In one scene, Thomas Hudson is shaving and thinking of all the good things that are made in Cuba, especially its excellent 90 proof alcohol. It is one of the few passages in which the island is praised.

The ceiba tree at Finca Vigía, mis-spelt seibo, also rates a mention. Thomas Hudson stands near it, holding his coat and waiting for his car. He gazes at the leaves and twigs that carpet the ground; the tree is old. Its branches are barren most of the year. Elsewhere, there is a scene in which Thomas Hudson handles a Mannlicher Schoenauer .256: the very one that can still be seen at Finca Vigía.

Hemingway's cat, Boise, also appears in the novel. Thomas Hudson purrs with her and talks to her as though she were a woman. In fact, Boise was not at Finca Vigía during the war years; she lived there much later and was Hemingway's favourite cat. She was part Persian, part Creole. When she died in 1966, the Finca Vigía employees followed the tradition started by Hemingway: they wrap-

ped her in a piece of cloth and buried her near the dining-room door. At least 50 cats must be buried there.

Hemingway also describes the house itself, a strange, silent place with no women or children in it. Only a neurotic chauffeur and a negro valet moving about as noiselessly as the cats.

Despite his enthusiasm and his professionalism, and although he had a thousand written pages of *Islands in the Stream*, Hemingway found it hard going and was never able to complete even this first section of the trilogy. No one knows exactly when he gave up or why the other two parts were never begun.

In 1961, Mary Hemingway obtained permission from the Cuban government to remove the paintings that had hung on the walls of Finca Vigía, as well as a number of manuscripts, including that of *Islands in the Stream*, which had been placed in a safe-deposit box at the National Bank of Cuba. In May 1970 Scribners announced publication of the book. It is impossible to tell how much editing went into the final version, although, his publisher, Charles Scribner Jr, claimed that the cuts were only those that Hemingway himself would have made.

Islands in the Stream is the darkest of all his works. And it is almost his own story.

CHAPTER EIGHT

FINCA VIGÍA

TIME STANDS STILL

*The tower at Finca Vigía, built in 1947. On the first
floor is the cats' home, on the second floor the
bathroom, and on the top floor a work place and a
library of military books.*

The areca palms, the ferns, the coral trees. The
swimming pool where quails came to drink and
where Ava Gardner used to swim naked. The
white tower where he retired to write. The field
where his baseball team won championships. It
was paradise. The home of a solitary artist. A
man who was sometimes cheerful but more
often melancholy. A legendary place. Paradise
was lost here at Finca Vigía, San Francisco de
Paula, Cuba.

Waldo Pierce painted the portrait in April 1929, at Key West. Pierce was a friend of John Reed and a veteran, like Hemingway, of the First World War. Hemingway may comb his hair like the portrait, but it serves only to emphasize the time that has passed.

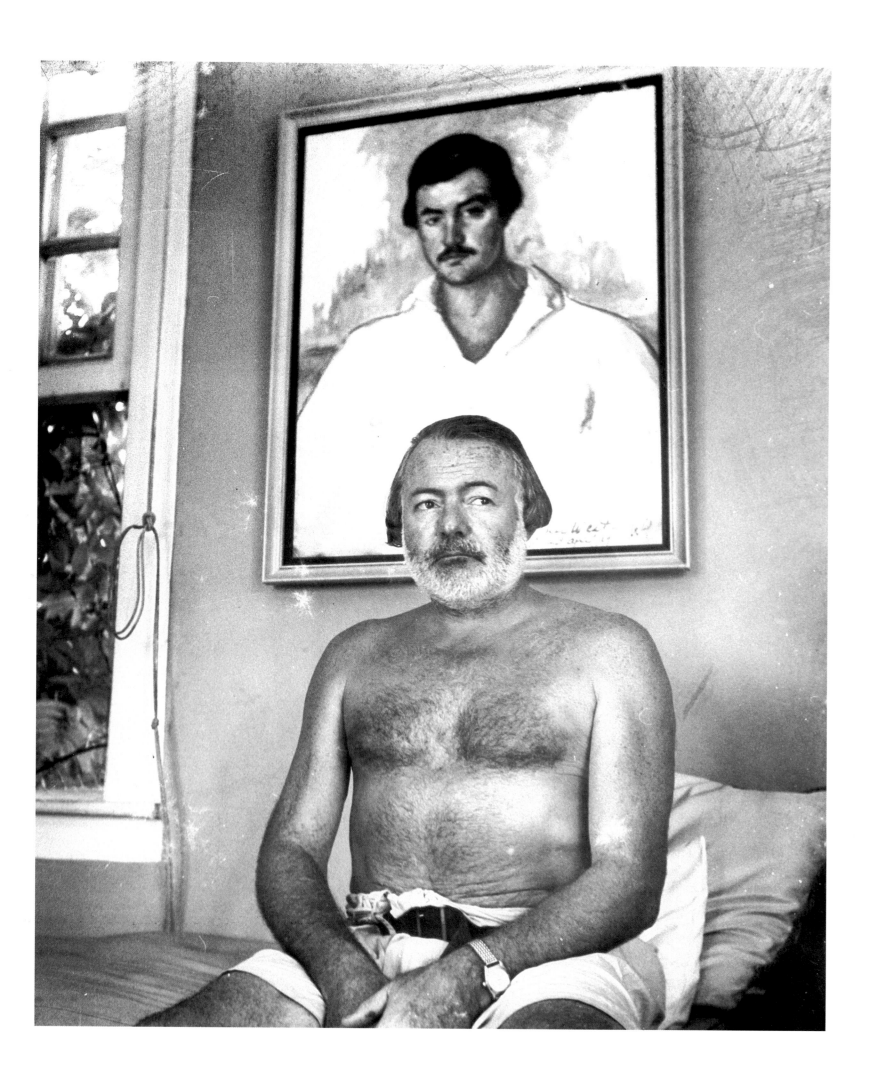

The village of San Francisco de Paula grew up around a
hermitage, built in the eighteenth century by a colonist from
the Canaries called Agustin de Arocha. Hemingway chose
to settle here, at Finca Vigía, and stayed for 21 years. The terrain
is uneven, with a hill to the north, where the narrow
Río Luyanó flows. It is 20 minutes from Havana and 10 miles
from the sea.

In the nineteenth century, the Spanish army installed an observation post on this site, providing the name – La vigía, the look-out – and the foundations for Finca Vigía. Protected by clumps of sweet-smelling lippia, arecas and other palm trees, here is Ernest Hemingway's Cuban fortress.

The living room at Finca Vigía. His favourite armchair is the one on the right. In the far left-hand corner is the old Capehart record-player, still in perfect working order. The record collection contains 900 discs and reveals great eclecticism: Cole Porter and Bach, Beethoven and Eddie de Lange, the songs of the International Brigade and Jerome Kern, Brahms and the music of the Navaho and Sioux Indians, Irving Berlin and beguines from Martinique, country music and Manuel de Falla, Albeniz and a recording of the Constitution of the United States. On the walls are two canvases by Roberto Domingo and a reproduction of the 'Don Manuel Osorio Manrique de Zúniga' by Goya. The only visible trophy: a brown stag from Wyoming, killed in 1930.

163

It became a habit: when he was reading in the evenings, Hemingway would stretch out his hand and take a bottle 'by the neck'. He devised this table-bar himself. The mixtures he drank were also often original recipes. Although the contents have been replaced by coloured water, the bottles themselves are original: Gordon's gin, Campari, Bacardi, Picard vermouth and White Horse whisky.

The furniture was chosen by Mary, but Martha bought the plant-fibre carpet in the Philippines in 1941. The radio is the transoceanic Zenith that Hemingway took with him on fishing trips, to the Cerro Hunting Club or on safari. On the wall is the head of a Grant gazelle. Hemingway added this specimen to his collection on the slopes of Kilimanjaro, near the village of Laitokitok.

The stamp bears the inscription 'I never write letters, Ernest Hemingway', and was intended to put off autograph hunters and people asking for advice. He never used it. Hemingway first used the Royal portable when working on For Whom the Bell Tolls. American collectors have offered up to $50,000 for it. He used the English-Spanish dictionary, compiled by Manolo Velázquez de la Cadena, published in 1942 by Wilcox Follewt, to draft the short speeches of thanks he was obliged to give at Cuban ceremonies paying him tribute. For example: 'For a solitary man, I have enough friends. But a man who does not master a language should take care not to speak it, even in his home.' The large blue book, titled Aerosphere and published in 1939, describes aeroplane engines of the time. But it had a more practical, and more regular, function – as a doorstop.

The lizard was found wounded at the Finca. Hemingway took it in and saved its life. When it died – of old age – he preserved it in formalin. He bought the Stetson hat in Nairobi in 1953, during his second African safari. The clipboard has paper marked with the Finca Vigía emblem (see page 187) and the two improvised paperweights are the swords from a white marlin (left) and a flying marlin. The fibre and wool doll is one of Hemingway's African fetishes. Who was the object of the black magic intended to bring the victim impotence and death? Faced with a writer in possession of such powers, no critic was safe from surprises.

In 1933–4, on his first safari, Hemingway killed two lions. Their skulls lie in the guest room, called the Venetian Room, at Finca Vigía. The funeral mask was brought back from the second safari in 1953–4. It belongs to the Makonde tribe and is decorated with human hair on the head and the eyebrows. 'Dr Hemorrhoid' was able to set up a dispensary with the medicine and first-aid equipment he carried with him.

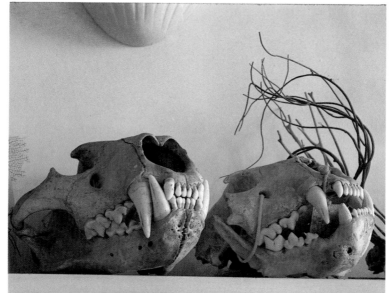

Hemingway's bedroom. The bed, which he rarely used because he slept with Mary, was somewhere to throw mail and the latest magazines. This is where he often came to work. Although a room in the tower was specially set aside for his writing, he found the place too quiet and preferred to work with the small sounds of the household around him. On the left-hand wall is the impala that he killed in Kenya in 1933. On the facing wall is the roan antelope he hunted down in the mountains in central eastern Tanganyika that same year.

Other views of Hemingway's bedroom. Barefoot or just in moccasins, Hemingway would stand in front of the bookcase on which perched his portable Royal. The small kudu skin that covered the floor at this spot was removed in 1986 because it had been worn out. The first drafts of his work were made in longhand and it was only when he began to revise text that it was transferred to the typewriter. The bookcase contains his works published in various languages. The stick was cut from a vine called qüira. He took it on his nocturnal rounds of Finca Vigía.

The famous eyeshade. Hemingway did not only use it to protect himself from the tropical sun, he also wore it when he was writing in the cool shade of his room.

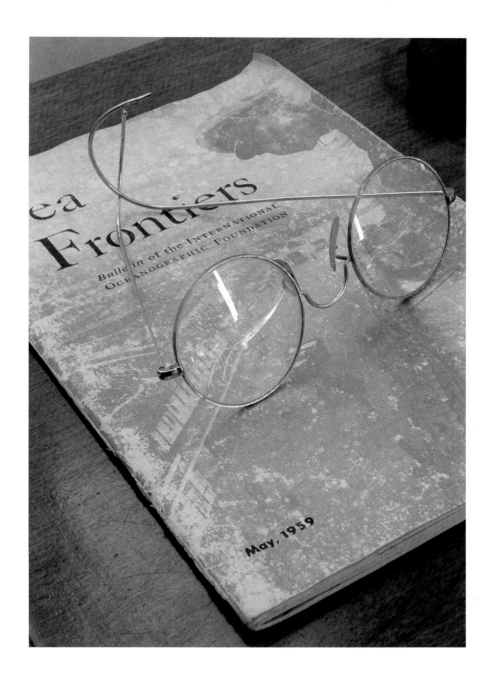

Hemingway read – as well as roamed – about the sea. The austere wire-rimmed spectacles gave the rugged seaman a scholarly look.

Indoor and garden shoes. He always went sockless in the moccasins.

Two of Hemingway's favourite cats: Boise, who appears in Islands in the Stream, *inspects the moccasin on the left, while Ambroise looks at the photographer.*

In August 1961, a few weeks after Hemingway's death, Mary
offered Fidel Castro Ernest Hemingway's favourite weapon, a
1903 Austrian Mannlicher Schoenauer .256. Today, it is kept
where he used to place it in his room. The tough guide in The
Short Happy Life of Francis Macomber, *Harry Street in* The
Snows of Kilimanjaro, *Mister Pop in* Green Hills of Africa *and
Thomas Hudson in* Islands In the Stream *used such a rifle. On
the desk is the collection of African wooden statuettes acquired
by Hemingway at Machakos, near Nairobi. On the wall is the
head of the wild buffalo that he added to his trophies during his
first safari. The photograph above shows the proud hunter,
posing with the kill in Tanganyika, 1934.*

An African figurine carved from the antler of a stag decorates a windowsill in the dining room at Finca Vigía. The crystal inkwell contains two keys, one from a room at the Ritz, the other from a cabin on board the liner Normandie, some penknives and a feather from an American vulture. The short sword is one of those worn by the Alalem warriors, a Masai tribe from the south of Kenya and the north of Tanganyika. The curved Arab dagger dates from the nineteenth century. Winchester cartridges and near them on the work table is a small personal collection of ammunition taken from German troops during the Second World War. Hemingway's favourite belt.

The miniature mandolin is made from the hard shell of a vegetable. The pegs are bone and the resonating chamber is inlaid with mother-of-pearl. In a cupboard are blank forms and writing materials. Under the glass-top of Hemingway's worktable is an alcohol consumer's permit, issued in the state of Idaho and tucked inside a plastic cover bearing an advertisement for Early Times whisky.

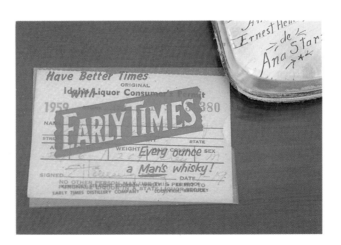

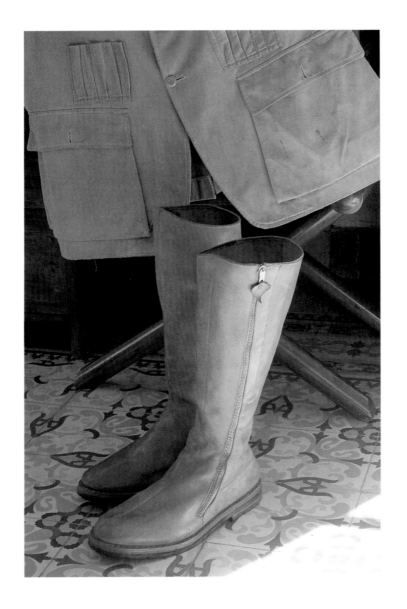

The well-worn leather jacket withstood the rigours of hunting in the mountains around Sun Valley, Idaho, and the plains of Africa. The safari jacket and boots he wore during his second African trip, in 1953–4. The cartridges are Western, Rem. Umc. super-X, calibre 6.5 and 20 mm which he never used.

The dining room. On the table are the two modern, factory-made, French reflecting lamps which gave Mary much pleasure. The room is decorated with the heads of two prong horns, or American antelopes, shot by Hemingway in 1939 and 1941 in Idaho. Sinsky was a frequent guest at the Hemingways' table.

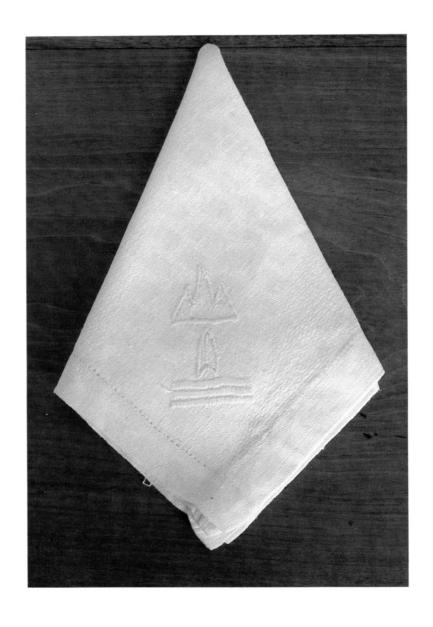

The emblem of Finca Vigía. The symbol at the top represents the three 'mountains' of Paris – Montparnasse, Montmartre and the Montagne Sainte-Geneviève – as well as the three hills of Finca Vigía. The arrow head below is borrowed from the Ojibwa tribe, whose territory covered the north of Michigan and Minnesota, where Hemingway spent part of his childhood. And the horizontal stripes at the bottom represent the rank of captain awarded both to Mary and Hemingway during the Second World War.

The library. On the right-hand side of the entrance is a plate by Picasso, decorated with a bull's head in relief and acquired by the Hemingways in 1957. On the same wall is another bull's head, made in wicker and bought in Spain. In the foreground is the desk made from majagua, a precious wood from Cuba, the work of the cabinetmaker Francisco Pasos Castro. On the left-hand side of the entrance is a Ruano Llopis poster announcing a bullfight at San Sebastián in 1927.

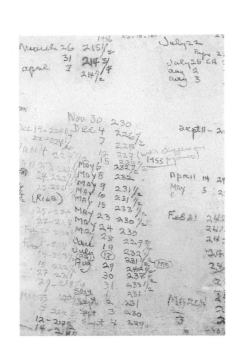

A private place. Hemingway watched his weight and, from time to time, checked his pulse. When recording the results, he used the same type of carpenter's pencil that he adopted for writing the first drafts of his novels.

*An American banknote, originally called a
'short-snorter' when signed as a souvenir by
several people who had crossed the Pacific or
the Atlantic by plane. The signatures have faded
with time. When Ernest Hemingway went to
China in 1941, transoceanic flights were still
quite uncommon.*